LATIN CAN BE FUN

LATIN CAN BE FUN

FACETIAE LATINAE

A Modern Conversational Guide

Sermo Hodiernus Antique Redditus

Translated by PETER NEEDHAM
from a German original by
GEORG CAPELLANUS

Illustrations by ROD McLEOD

SOUVENIR PRESS

First British edition published 1975 by Souvenir Press Ltd,
95 Mortimer Street, London W1N 8HP
and simultaneously in Canada by
J. M. Dent & Sons (Canada) Ltd,
Ontario, Canada

ISBN 0 285 62161 0

Set in Times 9 on 10½ pt. and
printed in Great Britain by Richard Clay (The Chaucer Press), Ltd,
Bungay, Suffolk

PREFACE TO THE ENGLISH EDITION

Throughout the book I have made such alterations as seemed appropriate for the English edition, and in general I have tried to present the material in an English rather than a German context. But some sections have been more radically altered; thus the section on **Politics** is almost entirely new, and that on **Sport** has been expanded to include a few items on cricket among other games. The **Geographical Appendix** has been largely recast as has the section entitled **Proverbial Expressions.** There are additional sections on the **Royal Family**, the **Peerage, Baronetage and Knightage** and **Military and Civil Decorations.** For this new material I am indebted to Mr J. G. Griffith who gave me access to the archives of the Public Orator at Oxford. His predecessor as Public Orator, Mr C. G. Hardie, with equal kindness vetted the new items in the section on **Sport,** and I am particularly grateful to my colleague, Mr D. P. Simpson, for looking over the whole manuscript and making many valuable suggestions.

PETER NEEDHAM

FROM THE PREFACE TO THE TENTH EDITION

The pseudonym Capellanus conceals the identity of a schoolmaster named Johnson from Saxony. Once on the staff of the grammar school at Plauen in Vogtland, he gave up teaching in order to become editor of the local newspaper. We are indebted to him for a similar little book entitled *Sprechen Sie Attisch?* (Do you speak Attic Greek? A modern phrase-book in colloquial Ancient Greek) which was published by the same publisher under the pseudonym Joannides.

Both works enjoy considerable success and keep appearing in new editions. Without doubt they owe much of their popularity to their agreeable and innocent humour. It is with amused surprise that one sees modern expressions such as *Münchner Allgemeine Zeitung*, *Waltz*, *Polka* and *Cheers! Here's to your health!* in somewhat stiff and formal Classical garb. At the same time one feels admiration for the linguistic knowledge and skill with which the task is carried out.

HANS LAMER

FROM THE PREFACE TO THE THIRTEENTH EDITION

Classical Latin as taught in schools is the basis of the vocabulary and sentence structure. When Classical words were not available words borrowed from Greek have been used in so far as these were already current in ancient Rome; otherwise silver Latin or late Latin words, and only in cases of emergency derivatives from Classical Latin words or short paraphrases mostly in keeping with Bacci's suggestions in *Lexicon eorum vocabulorum, quae difficilius Latine redduntur* (Rome-Vatican, 4th. edition 1963), a work of scholarly precision not available to my predecessors.

LUDWIG SPOHR

Some Hints on Pronunciation

ă as in cap
ā as in rather
ae as in sigh
ĕ as in vet
ē as in Beethoven (German)
ĭ as in flip
ī as in sleep
ŏ as in rot
ō as in Boot (German)
ŭ as in put
ū as in tool
g and c are hard. s is never pronounced as z (e.g. in nose).

In Latin polysyllabic words are stressed on the penultimate syllable if this is long; otherwise on the propenultimate syllable, provided that there is one. A syllable is long either if it contains a long vowel or it if ends in at least two consonants, but if the first of these consonants is a mute and the second is either *l* or *r*, a syllable containing a short vowel is short, e.g. *impetro* with the stress on the propenultimate syllable. In the text uncommon words with a long vowel in the penultimate syllable are marked with a long sign; occasionally the short sign is also used to remove any doubt.

TABLE OF CONTENTS

Speaking Latin	**de Latine loquendo**
Do you speak Latin?	*lŏquĕrisne lingua Latina?* (*cf.* Nepos, *Milt.* 3, 2).
Do you know Latin?	*scisne Latine?*
I understand it a little.	*haud multum scio.*
So, so.	*sic satis.*
Well then, let's have a conversation in Latin.	*age sīs* (= *si vis*) *Latine collŏquamur.*
Yes, by all means.	*age sānē.*
I should like to talk to you in Latin provided that you have the time and the inclination.	*stŭdĕo Latine tecum loqui, si modo tibi est otium et si vis* (*cf. Cic. Part. orat. 1, 1*).
I'm game.	*fiat.*
Do you understand what I say?	*intellegisne, quod dīco?*
I don't understand a single word.	*ego ne unum quidem verbum intellĕgo.*
You are speaking so fast that what you say is unintelligible.	*tam cĭtŏ loquĕris, ut non possint intellĕgi verba tua.*
When you speak slowly, I understand everything.	*quae tarde loquĕris, ea intellego omnia.*
You are not speaking loud enough.	*părum clārē loquĕris.*
How long have you been learning Latin?	*ex quo tempore Latine discis?* (*vel litteris Latinis operam das?*).
I started over a year ago.	*ante annum initium feci.*
Why are you learning it?	*quam ob rem id discis?*
In order to be able to read Latin books	*ut lĭbros Latine scriptos lĕgĕre possim*
and in order to be able to speak with those who know Latin.	*atque ut loquar cum iis, qui Latine sciunt.*
You have made very good progress.	*magnos fecisti progressus.*

I am delighted at your praise. *laude tua gaudio sum affectus magno.*

You must speak Latin whenever you have the opportunity. *Latine te loqui oportet, quotienscumque occasio data erit.*

But I'm afraid that I am making mistakes. *at metuo, ne vitiose loquar.*

On the whole you are speaking correctly. *satis recte loquĕris.*

You must speak Latin whenever you have the opportunity

How did you learn it? *quo pacto didicisti?*

I taught myself. *sine magistro didici.*

There's no need for you to be afraid. *non est cur metuas.*

You speak Latin well (very well). *bene (pérbĕne) Latine loquĕris.*

For various reasons it's worth the effort to learn Latin. *Latine discere variis ex causis operae pretium est.*

But what about you? *sed quid tu?*

I learned Latin at school, but the teaching wasn't good.	*in schola Latine didici, neque vero bona usus sum institutione.*
The way you are speaking is incorrect.	*vitiosus est sermo tuus.*
Your Latin reeks of the kitchen.	*sermo tuus (Latinus) culīnam redŏlet.* *Latinitate culinaria utĕris.*
On the other hand my brother knows very many modern languages.	*at frater meus plurimas scit linguas recentiores.*
He has a sound mastery of French, Italian, Spanish, Portuguese, Danish, Swedish, Dutch and English.	*Francogallica, Italica, Hispanica, Lusitanica, Danica, Suetica, Hollandica, Anglica sunt ei notissimae.*
He has also studied Anglo-Saxon.	*etiam Anglo-Saxonicam didicit.*
He has even learned Sanskrit on top of that.	*quid, quod linguam Sanscriticam addidicit?*

Good Weather	**de bona tempestate**
The weather is very nice today.	*sudum est hŏdie.*
Yes, it is really marvellous weather.	*est caelum mire serenum.*
Look how tempting it is!	*vide, ut tempestas arrideat!* (*Lucret. 2, 32*) or *vide blandos soles!* (*Ov. F. 1, 157*).
It is neither too hot nor too cold.	*neque aestus est neque frigus.*
The sun shines bright.	*caelum est splendidissimum.*
Nowhere is there a cloud to be seen.	*nulla usquam nubecula conspicitur.*
The air is clear and dry.	*caelum serenum est et siccum.*
It's a wonderful autumn day.	*caelum autumnale mirum in modum serenum est.*
I feel like going out.	*in animo habeo exire domo.*

If you feel like going for a walk, I should like to join you.	*si deambulare libet, non recuso.*
One must definitely make the most of the present weather.	*plane videtur hoc utendum caelo.*
The weather has stopped me going out for a few days.	*caelum me aliquot dies a publico cohibuit.*
We might take a few friends with us.	*asciscendi sunt nonnulli amici.*
Right. Just tell me whom you would like.	*fiet, modo* (= *dummodo*) *dicas, quos velis.*
How about Hugo?	*quid, si Hugonem?*
If you would like that, we'll take him with us, and we'll make Gustav come too.	*si videtur, eum asciscemus et Gustavum adiungemus.*

Bad Weather — de mala tempestate

It is really frightfully hot!	*est ingēns aestus!*
No wonder as the longest days are here!	*nec mirum, cum sit solstitium aestivum!*
If the heat is at all oppressive, let's keep the sun out with the help of the venetian blinds.	*volubilibus fenestrarum tegulis solem excludamus, si quid offendat aestus.*
The sun is scorching.	*sol urit.*
The sky is overcast.	*caelum nubibus obducitur.*
There are dark clouds in the sky.	*nubibus caelum obscuratur.*
The sun has gone. It's becoming damp.	*sol abiit. umēscit caelum.*
The atmosphere is sticky and oppressive.	*aer umĭdus est et crassus.*
It looks very much like rain.	*caelum admŏdum pluvium videtur esse; pluvia impendet.*
We shall soon have rain.	*imbres immĭnent. imber instat.*
A storm is on the way.	*tempestas cooritur.*
There's the first drop of rain!	*en haec prima gutta imbris!*

It's raining harder now.	*iam vehementius pluit; ruit imber.*
The rain's here to stay.	*imber tĕnet.*
It's raining buckets.	*urceatim pluit.*
There's a flash of lightning!	*iam fulgŭrat!*

The official weather forecasts are usually wrong

Listen! Thunder!	*tonat! audisne?*
The lightning has struck.	*cecĭdit fulmen.*
It has struck a tree.	*arborem fulmen tetigit.*
It's raining less hard.	*imber remittit.*
The storm is over.	*tempestas abiit.*
The wind is veering to the West (South-West, North-West, North, East, South).	*ventus se vertit in Favonium* (*Africum, Caurum, aquilonem, Eurum, austrum*).
The wind has dropped.	*ventus cecĭdit* (*vel cessavit*).
The sun is shining again.	*denuo nunc sol est.*

Do you see the rainbow? — *videsne arcum caelestem?*

We shall have good weather for our journey. — *tempestatem idoneam nanciscemur ad iter faciendum.*

The official weather forecasts are usually wrong. — *tempestatis futurae praedictiones publicae plerumque falsae sunt – non vero comprobantur eventu.*

What's the time? — quota hora?

What time is it? — *hora quota est? / quid horae est?*

It's three. — *tertia* (*nomin.*).

It is two o'clock. — *secunda* (*hora*) *est.*

It is ten minutes past two. — *decem minūtae nunc sunt post secundam.*

It is two minutes to nine. — *duae minūtae nunc sunt ante nonam.*

I don't think it has struck five yet. — *nondum quinta sonuit, credo.*

Oh no, it is long past. — *immo iamdudum praeteriit.*

It will soon be six. — *haud longe sexta abest.*

It will strike six any moment. — *instat hora sexta.*

You will soon hear it striking six. — *mox sextam audies.*

At what time will you fetch me? — *ad quam horam me abdūces?*

At ten, before the heat of the sun becomes too strong. — *ad decimam, priusquam invalescat aestus solis.*

I'll be there. — *curabitur.*

How many minutes more until three o'clock? — *quot minūtis nunc abest hora tertia?*

Five seconds. — *quinque punctis.*

Do you have a watch (pocket-watch) on you? — *habesne horologium* (*hor. portabile*)*?*

Yes. I always carry a watch on me. — *habeo. semper enim horologium mecum porto.*

Does it keep proper time?	*rectēne metītur?*
Yes, it is most accurate.	*rectissime, ut nihil supra.*
My watch is always slow.	*at meum horologium solet retardari.*
I forget to wind it up.	*intendere obliviscor.*
I set my watch every day in time with the radio.	*ita cottidie horologium meum ordĭno, ut cum horologio radiophonico congruat.*
Can you tell me the exact time?	*poterisne, quo momento temporis simus, pro certo dicere?*
It is exactly a quarter past two.	*secunda nunc ipsum est et quadrans.*
Then I still have fifteen minutes.	*etiamnunc igitur mihi vacat per quindecim minutas.*
We don't eat before eight o'clock, sometimes not even until nine.	*non cenamus ante octavam a meridie horam, nonnunquam nonam.*
I must go home at half past two.	*domum mihi abeundum est secunda hora et dimidia.*
Do you hear the clock just striking?	*audisne horam nunc ipsum?*
Didn't you hear it striking?	*nonne campānae vocem audivisti?*
The bell has struck twelve.	*hora duodecima audita est.*
I think that your watch is fast.	*currit ocius, credo, horologium tuum.*
My watch has stopped; it needs winding.	*substitit horologium meum; cursus enim suos absolvit.*

In Time — in tempore

You will have to wait a long time for that to happen.	*ad kalendas Graecas id fiet.*

NB: Since the Greeks had no *Kalends*, *ad kalendas Graecas* comes to mean never (a popular idiom among the Romans).

Circumstances do not permit it.	*res non sinit.*
There is still time.	*etiamnunc tempus est.*
I have no time at present. (I can't get away now.)	*in praesentia non est otium. nunc mihi haud vacat.*
Why are you in such a hurry, John?	*cur tantopere curris, Iohannes?*
I'll be beaten if I don't arrive on time.	*quia, nisi adfuero in tempore, actum erit de pelle mea.*
You have nothing to be afraid of in this respect.	*hac quidem ex parte nihil est periculi.*
It's only just gone seven.	*modo praeteriit septima.*
Look at the watch. The hand hasn't reached the half hour yet.	*inspice horologium, gnomon nondūm attigit horam mediam.*
But watches are sometimes wrong.	*at horologia mentiuntur nonnunquam.*
Mine is correct.	*meum non mentītur.*
We'll arrive in time.	*tempori (temperi) veniemus.*
We are late.	*serius venīmus.*
A little late – very late.	*paulo serius – serius aliquanto.*

Other Expressions of Time — de temporibus aliis

How many years ago?	*quot sunt annī?*
Years? Hardly ten months ago!	*quot anni? vix decem sunt menses!*
It's still less than a full year since the wedding.	*nondum annus expletus est a nuptiis.*
It's hardly three months since that happened.	*nondum quartus (ab ea re) mensis est.*
It's already light.	*iam lucet.*
Evening is coming on.	*vesperascit.*
Why do you go out so early in the morning?	*cur tam mane egredĕris?*
Very early in the morning.	*bene mane. multo mane.*

This morning, tomorrow morning, yesterday morning.	*hodie mane, cras mane, heri mane.*
The following morning.	*postridie mane.*
Do you come home so late in the evening?	*tam vesperi domum revertĕris?*
Very late in the evening.	*pervesperi.*
Yesterday evening.	*heri vesperi.*
He has been there long enough.	*satis iam ibi fuit.*
The day before yesterday, the day after tomorrow, in a year's time.	*nudius tertius, perendie, ad annum.*
Twenty years ago today.	*abhinc viginti annos (vel annis).* *ante (hos) viginti annos.*
Twice hourly, daily, weekly, monthly, yearly.	*bis in hora, in die, in hebdomăde, in mense, in anno.*
In the last three years.	*proximo triennio.*
The days of the week:	*dies Solis, Lunae, Martis, Mercurii, Iovis, Veneris, Saturni.*
At Easter.	*paschali tempore*
At Whitsun.	*diebus Pentecostalibus.*
At Christmas.	*die natali Christi.*
In the summer holidays, Easter holidays, Christmas holidays.	*feriis aestivis, paschalibus, brumalibus.*
On a public holiday.	*die nationis; die populi.*
On Mayday.	*die Laboris.*

You're joking! — iocose dicta

Is Charles in?	*Carŏlus estne domi?*
I'm not sure; I'll have a look.	*incertus sum; sed visam.*
Thank you, but I would prefer	*benigne; potius ipse ibo et ro-*

to go myself and ask him personally whether he feels like being in.	*gabo ipsum; velitne nunc esse domi.*
I would prefer to go myself and be my own messenger.	*ibo ipse potius, ut sim ipse mihi Mercurius.*
Hallo, Charles, are you at home?	*heus, Carŏle, esne domi?*
No!	*non sum!*
What cheek! Isn't that your voice I hear?	*impŭdens, nonne ego audio te loquentem?*
You are much more cheeky! Recently I believed your maid when she told me that you were not at home, and yet you refuse to believe me when I tell you myself.	*immo tu impudentior. nuper ancillae tuae credidi te non esse domi, nunc tu non credis mihi ipsi.*
Come off it! You're at it again.	*age, tuo more facis.*
You're just having a joke at my expense.	*nunc ludis tu quidem me.*
Don't think I haven't noticed that you're getting at me!	*non me fallit ista cavillatio!*
That simply must be a joke on your part.	*nunc plane ioco mecum agis.*
You're making fun of me.	*sum tibi risui (vel rideor a te).*
I'm only saying what I really think.	*loquor id, quod sentio.*
On my word of honour, it's the truth.	*dispeream, si quid fingo. ne vivam, si quid simulo.*
I mean what I say.	*bona fide loquor.* *non secus sentio ac loquor.*

Indignation — **de verbis indignantis**

Go to blazes!	*abi in malam rem!*
I can hardly keep my hands off you.	*vix tempero manibus.*

How very like you! (cf. p. 54).	*ut semper tui similis es!*
Does this annoy you?	*haec res male urit te?*
I can hardly say how much.	*sic, ut dici vix possit.*
What are you thinking of?	*quid hoc novae rei est?*
Stop joking!	*mitte iŏcos!* (also: *ioca*).
What kind of a man are you?	*quidnam tu hominis es?*
In heaven's name!	*pro Iuppiter!*
I'll make him pay for that!	*ego pol eum ulciscar probe!*
What's that supposed to mean?	*quae haec est fabula?*
You know very well!	*dixi tibi!*
Stuff and nonsense!	*fabulae!*
One might as well hang oneself.	*res redit ad restim* (rope)!
And you're taking offence too?	*etiam indignaris?*
I can hardly believe it.	*vix crediderim.*
What silly stuff!	*age, ineptē!*
Bad show!	*male factum!*
I am very disappointed.	*quanta de spe decĭdi!*
What's up?	*quid istuc quaeso?*
I don't like to hear that.	*male narras!* (*vel male dicis, dixisti*)
Do be quiet!	*tăce sodes!*
The devil take you!	*di te eradīcent!*
What story is he making up?	*quid ille narrat?*
Are you in your right mind?	*satin' sanus es?* (*sanusne es?* = *sanun' es?*)
Whatever am I to think of you?	*quaeso quid tu hominis es?*
Have you already forgotten what we discussed?	*iamne oblitus es, quid inter nos sit dictum?*
Remarkable!	*mira narras!*
What's that? What do you tell me?	*quid ais? quid audio?*
That sounds suspicious.	*timeo!*
I am beside myself with anger.	*prae iracundia non sum apud me!*
Restrain yourself, please!	*non tu te cohĭbes?*
What harm has he done you?	*quid in te fecit?*
That is shocking!	*o facinus indignum!*

I want him to remember me as long as he lives!	*is, dum vivat, meminerit mei!*
Please don't be so angry!	*minue vero iram!*

Greetings — de salutatione

Greetings	de salutatione
Hallo!	*salve!* *salvus sis!* *ave!*
Good-bye!	*vale!* *ave!*
Good morning, Father!	*salve, pater!*
Good morning, Mummy!	*salve, matercula!*
Good day, dear brother!	*salve, mi frater!*
Good morning, my dearest grandson!	*salve, dulcissime něpōs!*
Good night! (cf. p. 31)	*mollĭter cubes!*
My dear husband!	*mi vir!*
My dear wife!	*mea uxor!*
My sweetheart! My darling!	*cor(cŭlŭm) meum! mel(cŭlŭm) meum!*
Good evening, gentlemen!	*salvete pariter omnes!*
Here's Gustav! Splendid!	*Gustavum optime eccum!*
Good day, Sir!	*salve, bone vir!*
(Reply.) Good day to you, my dear Sir!	*salve tantundem mihi, carissime!*
Good day, your Excellency!	*salve, vir ornatissime (vel clarissime vel spectatissime)!*
You are welcome, Sir!	*salve tu quoque, bone vir!*
Nice to see you, my friend.	*salve multum, mi amice!*
Absolutely delighted to see you, my very dear friend.	*salve etiam atque etiam, amicorum ŏptime!*
I'm pleased to see you well.	*salvum te venire gaudeo!* *venire salvum volup est!* *gaudeo venisse salvum!* *salvum te advenisse gaudeo!*

Congratulations on your safe return!	*gratulor tibi de reditu tuo!*
Thank God that you're safely back!	*gratia Deo, quod nobis incolumis redīsti!*
How nice to meet you so conveniently!	*ego te mihi tam opportune obvium fieri gaudeo.*
You come at the right moment!	*opportune advĕnis!*
Please take a seat!	*assīde quaeso!*
Please sit down on the sofa (in the easy-chair).	*in lectulo* (*in cathĕdra molli*) *assīdito, si commodum erit.*
My brother sends his kindest regards.	*frater meus tibi me salutem multam voluit dicere.*
My mother and sister have asked me to pass on their best wishes.	*mater et soror tibi salutem me iusserunt dicere* (*impertiunt tibi multam salutem, Cic. ad Att. 2, 12, 4*).
Bless them!	*salvae sint!*

Rare Visits — de visitatione rara

We were just talking about you.	*de te sermo erat.*
I can well believe it, for on my way here my ears were burning violently, which makes me think that you weren't saying anything particularly nice about me.	*facile crediderim, nam mihi huc venienti mire flagrabant aures. unde conicio nihil magnifice de me fuisse praedicatum.*
Oh! no; we weren't saying anything that wasn't nice.	*immo nihil non bene.*
So I was wrong in my suspicion.	*vanum igitur fuit.* *nihil igitur est.*
You haven't been to see us for a year.	*iam annus est, ex quo nos invisisti.*

What's the reason for your not coming to see us for such a long time?	*quid causae est, cur tam diu nos non inviseris?* / *quid accidit, ut tam diu nos non adires?*
Why is it that you visit us so seldom?	*quid rei est, quod nos tam raro visis?*
What has prevented you from visiting us more often?	*quid obstitit, quominus viseres nos frequentius?*
Where have you been hiding all this time?	*ubi tu tam diu latuisti?*
The more often you come, the more welcome you will be.	*quo crebrius venies, eo mihi venies gratior.*
I'm a little annoyed with you.	*nonnihil ego tibi succenseo.* / *ego tibi subirascor.*
I have some reason to be angry with you.	*nonnihil est* (*vel habeo*), *quod tibi succenseam.*
What can that be? Please, tell me!	*quid est istud, obsecro?*
In what respect?	*quid ita?*
But why? Do tell me!	*quam ob rem tandem, oro?*
What have I done wrong?	*quid admisi sceleris?*
Because you don't think of us.	*quod nihil nos respĭcis.*
Because you visit us so seldom.	*quod raro nos revīsis.*
Because you don't bother about us (neglect us completely).	*quod nihil nos curas.* (*quod nos plane neglĕgis*).
Why do you make a point of avoiding our get-togethers?	*quid est causae, cur nostros circulos devītes?*
Don't you get tired of being alone so much?	*nonne taedium te capit solitudinis?*

Excuses — de excusatione

There's no reason for you to be angry with me;	*non est, quod mihi succenseas;*

for it's not my fault that I've been to see you less often.	*neque enim mea culpa accidit, ut te rarius viserem.*
It wasn't possible because I was too busy.	*non licuit mihi per occupationes.*
I was so busy that I wasn't able to pay you my respects.	*non patiebantur negotia, quibus involvebar, ut te salutarem.*
I was too busy to be able to do so.	*occupatior fui, quam ut possem.*
I hardly had a moment to myself.	*vix ipsi mihi fuit copia mei.*
Put it down to my work, not to me personally.	*negotiis meis ascrībes, non mihi.*
It wasn't possible because of my health (because of the bad weather).	*non licuit per valetudinem (per tempestatem).*
I accept your excuse, but only on condition that you don't make a habit of it.	*accipio excusationem tuam, sed hac lege, ne saepius ea utaris.*
You will be forgiven on condition that you try to make up what you have missed.	*hac lege mihi purgatus eris, si, quod cessatum est in officio (Liv. 45, 24, 7), sarcias.*

What can I do for you?	**quid vis?**
What brings you to me?	*quid me vis?*
I should like to have a word with you.	*paucis te volo.*
I should like to talk to you privately and in confidence.	*cupio tecum separatim colloqui familiarius.*
Tête-à-tête.	*arbĭtris remotis.* *sine arbitris.*
Tell me what you want.	*loquĕre, quid velis!*
Well, what can I do for you?	*cĕdo, quid vis faciam?*
What's up?	*quid est (rei)?*
Is it a business matter?	*numquid est negotii?*

No, I was just passing and looked in to see how you were.	*non ita, sed forte praeteriens intravi, ut viderem, quid tu ageres.*
How very kind!	*bene facis!*
May I offer you a glass of wine?	*licetne apponere vinum?*
I'm afraid that I must refuse.	*invītus nego.*
Or a glass of beer?	*cervesiam mavis?*
Thank you (accepting) or No, thank you (declining).	*benigne!*
I've promised to meet a man at eleven o'clock.	*pollicitus sum me hora undecima virum quendam conventurum esse.*
I'm sorry that you are in such a hurry.	*nollem te properare.*
I'll stay longer another time.	*alio tempore diutius adero.*

Farewell	**vale!**
I must say good-bye now.	*iubeo nunc te bene valere.*
It's time for me to go now; good-bye!	*iam me tempus alio vocat; tu valebis!*
I won't keep you any longer.	*non te diutius remorabor.*
Another time we'll talk (chat) about the matter more fully.	*alias latius loquemur (nugabimur vel confabulabimur).*
I still have a little shopping to do.	*nunc alio me vocant negotiŏla quaedam.*
I'm saying good-bye to you for two days.	*in hoc biduum valebis.*
Have a very good time!	*valeto quam optime!*
Look after yourself!	*da operam, ut sis prospera valetudine!*

NB: On taking leave the Romans usually asked the question: Can I do anything for you? *numquid vis?* to which the answer could be: *ut bene sit tibi!*

And the same to you!	*valebis tu quoque!* *tibi vicissim precor prosperam valetudinem!*
Remember me most kindly to your father.	*tu me patri tuo viro optimo magnopere commenda!* *fac me patri tuo quam commendatissimum facias!*
Give my kind regards to your mother and father and to any other friends you see.	*salutem dic matri et patri et si quem alium benevolentem viděris!*
Give my best wishes to your brother.	*nuntia fratri tuo salutem verbis meis!*
Send Charles my very best wishes.	*Carŏlum iubebis meis verbis salvere plurimum!*
And be sure to pass on my regards to Frederick too.	*Friderīcum item mea causa salutabis diligenter!*
Pass on my sincere greetings to them all.	*dic me omnibus omnia laeta precari!*
Give them all my best wishes.	*omnes meis verbis saluta!*
Shall I pass on any message to your family?	*ecquid tuis mandas per me?*
Send them my kindest regards.	*ut recte valeant!*
Heartfelt greetings to all, especially to my father.	*multam salutem omnibus, sed praecipue patri!*
Would you like me to remember you to anyone?	*suntne, quos per me tuo nomine velis salutatos?*
Yes, to anyone who asks after me.	*omnes, qui de me percontabuntur!*
I take my leave of you.	*me tibi commendo!* (*recommendo* is not a Latin word).
Don't keep me any longer.	*ne sis mihi iam mŏra!*
Farewell.	*vale!*
Good-bye until tomorrow.	*vale in crastĭnum!*

Good Wishes	**De faustis ominibus**
All the best to you!	*bene vale! bene valeto!*
And the same to you!	*et tu!*
Have a good journey and come back safe.	*bene ambŭla et redambula!*
Good luck!	*bene rem gere!*

Good luck!

I'll keep my fingers crossed.	*pollicem prĕmam!*
Enjoy your trip.	*sit iter laetum!*
My best wishes go with you.	*optimis* (*faustis*) *ominibus te prosequor.*
Keep well.	*cura, ut quam rectissime valeas!*
Enjoy yourself!	*bene sit tibi!*
Congratulations on your success.	*gratulor felicitati tuae!*

(*gratulari* always refers to an event that has already taken place, never to the future.)

All the best for the New Year!	*annum novum faustum tibi precor!* *omnia bona tibi precor in proximum annum!*
Happy New Year!	*annum novum faustum felicem!*

(Inscription on a small lamp in the state collection of sculpture in Dresden).

I wish you luck at the start of your enterprise.	*feliciter cedat, quod instituisti!* *feliciter exeat, quod aggressus es!* *bene vertat, quod agis!*
Have a good night's rest!	*precor tibi noctem placidam!* *contingat tibi felix somnus!*
I wish you a good night	*sit tibi fausta nox* (*cf. p. 24*).
Good night to one and all.	*valete omnes!*

Requests and Thanks	**de precibus et gratiis**
Please give me a knife.	*da mihi quaeso cultrum!*
Be so kind as to give me a fork.	*dato mihi fuscinulam, si commŏdum erit!*
May I ask you for a spoon?	*dato mihi cochlĕar, nisi molestum erit!*
Would you be so kind as to lend me your book?	*librum tuum, amabo, commoda mihi!*
You would be doing me a great favour if you lent me this book.	*pergratum mihi feceris, si hunc mihi librum commodaveris.*
Here it is.	*accipe!*
Many thanks, dear Charles.	*merito te amo, Carŏle!*
Thank you for letting me have the book.	*gratias ago, quod* (*vel bene facis, quod*) *hunc mihi librum commodasti.*
Would you like to do me a favour?	*ecquid gratum mihi facies?*

Very much.	*cupio.*
With pleasure! What do you want?	*faciam animo libenti. dic: quid est?*
What can I do for you?	*quid me vis facere?*
You are very kind.	*benigne facis!*
I'm very much obliged to you.	*gratiam habeo maximam!*
Thank you very much indeed.	*gratias tibi ago maximas!*
I'm most obliged to you for this kindness.	*amo te de istoc tuo officio!*
I'm most indebted to you for this favour.	*istoc beneficio tibi magnopere devinctus sum!*
Don't mention it.	*aufer mihi ista!*

Doing a favour	**de officiositate**
I beg you to keep this matter in mind.	*quaeso, ut haec res tibi cordi sit!*
I beg you most earnestly to concern yourself with this matter.	*etiam atque etiam rogo, ut haec res tibi sit curae!*
Please keep your eyes open where this is concerned.	*hac in re quaeso, ut advigĭles!*
For my sake take great care over this matter.	*curabis hanc rem mea causa diligenter!*
Yes, I'll do so for your sake.	*faciam tua gratia* (*vel in tuam gratiam*).
I'll do my utmost.	(*maxime*) *operam dabo.*
You've done me a favour in drawing my attention to it.	*gratum mihi fecisti, quod illud me monuisti.*
I'm much obliged to you for doing that.	*amo te, quod istuc fecisti.*
I feel myself very much indebted to you for your kindness.	*debeo tibi pro beneficio tuo.*
I'm most grateful to you, and	*equidem gratiam tibi et habeo*

will be so for as long as I live.	*et habebo, quoad vivam, maximam.*
I know how much I owe to your good-will towards me.	*video, quantum debeam tuo erga me studio.*
Forget about it!	*mitte!* (*vel desine!*)
You have no reason to thank me.	*non est, quod gratias agas.*

Blaming — **de culpa**

That's not fair of you.	*non aequum facis.*
What have I done wrong?	*quidnam commisi?*
It's not my (your) fault.	*non sum (es) in culpa.* *culpa non est mea (tua).* *non est culpa in me (te).*
I'm not to blame.	*ego careo culpa.* *extra culpam sum.* *ego absum a culpa.* *culpa vaco.*
That's my fault.	*haec mea culpa est.*
You are most to blame.	*tua summa culpa est.*
The fault is on your side.	*tu in vitio es.*
You are a stern judge.	*Cassianus iudex es.*

(L. Cassius Longinus Ravilla was well-known in Rome as a stern judge. Consequently on several occasions Cicero speaks of Cassius-like judges and verdicts.)

The reason why I didn't write to you was that I was ill.	*quominus ad te scriberem, morbus causa fuit.*
Pressure of work was the only reason why I wrote to you so seldom.	*quod rarius tibi scripsi, negotia mea causa fuerunt.*
What was the reason for that?	*quae causa fuit?* *quid causae fuit?*
I don't want to hold you up.	*non ero tibi in mŏra.* *per me nulla est mora.*

What held you up? — *quidnam tibi in mora fuit?*
You held us up. — *tu nobis in mora fuisti.*
Who (what) delayed you? — *quis (quid) te remoratus (-um) est?*

It was Max's fault that Maurice didn't finish the job. — *per Maximum stetit, quominus Mauricius rem conficeret.*
He did it on purpose. — *data (vel dedita) opera fecit.*
It's none of my business. — *res me nihil contingit.*
What others do doesn't concern me. — *quid alii faciant, ipsi viderint.*
That's not up to me. — *haec non sunt in manu nostra.*
To the best of my ability. — *quantum est situm in me.*

Forgiveness — **de venia**

I wish you would forgive him. — *ei ignōscas volo.*
Forgive me. — *ignōsce!*
Please, forgive me. — *obsĕcro mihi ignōscas!*
What have I done that's so terrible? — *quid ego tantum sceleris admisi?*
Everyone does it. — *vulgo faciunt!*
It's generally done. — *vulgo fit!*
That's life! — *ut sunt humana!*
What should I have done? — *quid facerem?*
My friends were in favour. — *sic amicis visum est!*
Everyone has his faults. — *sunt sua cuique vitia!*
We all have our moments of weakness. — *nemo est mortalium, qui sapiat omnibus horis.*
Don't get into a state. — *noli tumultuari!*
Don't get too angry. — *noli nimium stomachari!*

A Misfortune	**de fortuna adversa (vel calamitate)**
What's the matter?	*quid rei est?*
Why are you sighing?	*quid suspīras?*
Oh dear! Oh dear!	*perii!*

We all have our moments of weakness . . .

All my money has gone.	*universae pecuniae naufragium feci.*
Where did you lose it?	*ubĭnam?*
In London at Marble Arch station.	*Londinii in ferratae viae statione Arcus Marmorei.*
How did it happen?	*quī mălum hoc accidit?*
I don't know. It must be my bad luck.	*nescio, nisi forte sic erat in fatis meis.*
Please accept my sympathy.	*doleo vicem tuam!*

Honestly, I am sorry for you.	*ita me di amabunt, ut tui me miseret!*
Console yourself.	*bono animo es!* *bono animo fac sis!*
Don't take on so.	*noli te macerare!*
I'll help you out.	*ero auxilio tibi!*

Forms of Enquiry	**de quaerendi modis**
What nice thing has happened that you're smiling to yourself so sweetly?	*quid est bonae rei, quod tecum rides tam suaviter?*
I've just heard a very amusing story.	*fabellam modo audivi lepidissimam.*
I wonder what has gone wrong with him.	*demiror, quid huic evenerit mali.*
Tell me honestly:	*dic bona fide:*
what's your business with the boss?	*quid tibi cum rectore est negotii?* *quid ages cum rectore?*
I can't tell you.	*non possum tibi dicere.*
Nor is it very important.	*nec multum interest.*
You'll learn.	*scies.*
You didn't say?	*non tu dixisti?*
No.	*non dixi.*
Why not?	*quámobrem?*
Is that really so?	*satin' hoc certum est?*
Certainly. I've seen it with my own eyes.	*certum. his egomet oculis vidi.*
What's going on?	*quid est?*
Seriously?	*ain' tu?*
You're putting me on the rack. I'm bursting with impatience.	*ēnĕcas (summam in exspectationem me adducis).*
Understood? Yes, very well.	*intellextin'? – probe!*
I don't understand.	*non intellego!*

What do you think of Sophocles' Antigone?	*quid tibi Sophoclis Antigona?*
What's your opinion about . . .?	*quid iudicas de . . .?*
What do you feel about . . .?	*quid sentis de . . .?*
What's the meaning of this?	*quid hoc sibi vult?* *quid hoc rei est?*
If you want to know, I'll tell you.	*si scire vis, ego dicam.*
Tell me; please!	*dic, obsecro!*
But do you know what?	*at scin' quid, sodes?*
What next?	*quid?*
Do you understand?	*tenesne?*
This is so, isn't it?	*nōnne? – ain' tu?*
It isn't? Why not?	*non? quámobrem?*
Oh! How can you ask?	*vah, quid rogas?*
How come?	*quamobrem? quid ita?*
How did that happen?	*quid ita istuc?*
Well? (speak!).	*cĕdo!*
What's that you say?	*quid tu?*
What then?	*quid tum?*
Is it so?	*ităne?*
Really?	*sic factum?*
Why that? For I simply don't understand . . .	*quamobrem istuc? nam prorsum nihil intellego . . .*
Are you still in doubt about that?	*an dubium id tibi est?*
We can do without that.	*non est opus!*
Do without it?	*non opus est?*

Affirmative Answers	**de modis affirmandi**
That's quite credible (plausible).	*facile credo!*
What you say is probably true.	*verisimile dicis!*
That's not hard to credit.	*non difficile creditu est.*
Just as you say.	*ita, ut dicis!*

You must be right about that.	*istud tibi quis non credat?*
You're right there.	*recte iudicas!*
I'm well aware of that.	*bene scio! probe scio!* *non sum ignarus!* *non sum nescius!*
As far as I know.	*quantum scio. – quod sciam*
That's perfectly obvious.	*hoc in promptu est.* *in aperto hoc est!*
But what do you think?	*sed quid tu?*
That's self-evident.	*hoc ex se intellegitur!*
To be sure.	*sane!*
Quite right.	*probe!*
You know that it happened as I say?	*scis esse factum, ut dico?*
The devil take me if I lie.	*peream, si mentiar!*
Of course.	*quidni?*
Why not? By all means.	*quippĭni?*
How can you ask?	*rogas?*
You're not completely wrong.	*recte sane!*
I saw it for myself.	*hisce oculis vidi.*
Don't deny it.	*noli negare! ne negaveris!* (in colloquial Latin: *ne nega!*)
Could be.	*esto!*

Negative answers	**de modis negandi**
Is everything going according to plan?	*satin' omnia ex sententia?*
I wish it were.	*vellem quidem!*
No.	*non ita.*
Rubbish.	*nihil dicis!*
Definitely not.	*non inquam!*
On no account	*non hercle vero!*
You won't convince me of that.	*non possum addūci, ut id credam.*

Is it possible? Impossible! You can't be serious.	*quid ais?*
I've not forgotten.	*memini!*
That's what I think.	*sic arbitror!*
I understand.	*intellego!*
You have a point there.	*aliquid dicis!*
Pleased to hear it.	*audio!*
No wonder.	*non mirum!* *nec mirum!* *quid mirum?* *minime mirum id quidem!*
You've hit the nail on the head.	(*rem*) *acu tetigisti!*
Naturally.	*scilicet!*
How right you are.	*haud erras!*
He is definitely at home.	*mirum, ni domi est.*
If I'm not mistaken, here he is.	*nisi me animus fallit, hic ille est.*
To be sure.	*ĕdĕpol!*
I said at once that it was he.	*dixi equidem ilĭco eum esse.*
Could be.	*fortasse!*
Nearly.	*propemŏdum!*
You'll see.	*ipsa re experiēris!*
Very well.	*sit ita! – esto! – fiat!*
But that's perfectly natural.	*minime mirum id quidem!*
That's as clear as day.	*hoc luce clarius!*
May one see the photograph?	*licetne videre imaginem luce impressam?*
Yes. (Yes, of course.)	*licet.* (*licet maxime!*).
That's how it is. I admit it.	*ita res est, fateor!*
That's how it is.	*sic est!*
Certainly.	*certo!*
Just as I told you.	*dixi!*
You're joking.	*garris!*
Not at all.	*minime!*
You're out of your mind.	*delīras!*
So are you.	*tu nihilo minus!*

I protest most vigorously.	*reclāmo, quantum possum!*
That's easily said.	*nihil est dictu facilius!*
It's all very well for you to talk.	*dixti pulchre!*
No need.	*nihil opus!*
I don't know.	*nescio. – ignoro.*

I protest most vigorously

Parentheses	**de interpositionibus**
In brief.	*ne multa –* *quid plura?* *sed quid opus est plura?*
To put it briefly.	*ut paucis complectar:*
To put it more clearly.	*ut planius dicam:*
But that is beside the point.	*sed hoc nihil ad rem!*
But to return to the point.	*sed ad rem!*
Believe me.	*mihi crede* (better than: *crede mihi*)!

Rest assured . . .	*persuade tibi . . .*
Please rest assured . . .	*velim tibi ita persuadeas . . .*
According to my deepest convictions.	*ex animi mei sententia.*
If I'm not mistaken.	*nisi fallor. nisi me fallit. nisi res me fallit. nisi animus me fallit.*
If I'm not completely mistaken.	*nisi omnia me fallunt.*
You grasp my meaning?	*tenes, quid dicam?*
– which God forbid! –	*quod Deus avertat!* *quod Deus prohibeat!*

How old? — **qua aetate?**

Tell me honestly: how old are you?	*dic bona fide* (*vel sincere, sine fraude*)*: quot annos natus es? vel qua aetate es?*
I'm fifteen years old.	*quindecim annos natus sum.*
I'm in my sixteenth year.	*sextum decimum annum ago.*
I'm over eighteen.	*maior sum annis duodeviginti.*
Is your brother older than you?	*fraterne tibi antĕit aetate?*
No, I'm older than he is.	*immo ego ei* (*aetate*) *antecēdo.*
He's a year and a half younger than I am.	*anno et sex mensibus minor est quam ego.*
He's not yet fourteen.	*minor est quattuordecim annis natu.*
He looks almost as old as you.	*aequalis prope tui videtur esse.*
Is your grandmother still alive?	*vivitne avia tua?*
Yes, indeed.	*vivit.*
Is she very old?	*estne grandis natu?*
She was seventy-five last week.	*hac proxima hebdomăde septuaginta quinque annos complevit.*
She's as old as that?	*illa tanta natu?*

She's getting on towards eighty.	*annum ingressa est octogesimum.*
That's a great age.	*magnam dicis senectutem!*
She's still very active.	*etiamnunc vivĭda est.*
When is your birthday?	*quando tibi natalis dies est?*
On September 15th.	*die quinto decimo (mensis) Septembris.*
How old will you be then?	*quot annos tum conficies?*
I'll be fifteen then.	*quindecim tum annos natus ero.*
How old do you think I am?	*quid aetatis ego tibi videor?*
You are forty.	*quadraginta annos natus es.*
I'm passed forty-six.	*quadragesimum sextum annum excessi (vel egressus sum).*
Your uncle is beginning to age.	*avunculus tuus senescit.*
His hair is turning grey.	*canescit.*
His hair is almost as white as snow.	*eius capilli nivĕo fere sunt colore.*
He is as old as the hills.	*ad summam senectutem pervēnit.*

Physical Appearance	**de corporis specie**
A very good-looking boy.	*scitus admodum puer!*
He has his father's nose and eyes while his forehead and chin resemble his mother's.	*nasus et oculi patrem refĕrunt; frons et mentum matrem exprĭmunt.*
I hardly recognised you.	*vix te agnovi.*
Have I aged so much in two years?	*adeone consenui biennio?*
On the contrary, you look much younger because you've shaved off your beard.	*immo aetate multo minor videris, quod barbam totondisti.*
You've come back fatter (taller).	*obesior (procerior) redīsti.*

You were clean-shaven when you went away, but you've come back wearing a little beard.	*imberbis abieras, redīsti barbatulus.*
He is short-sighted.	*oculis non satis prospicit.*
He wears spectacles.	*oculos arte adiŭvat.* *perspicillum fert.*

He is short-sighted

Do you see Mr Miller over there with his bride?	*videsne Molinarium illum cum spōnsa?*
Yes.	*video.*
Who is his bride?	*quaenam est eius spōnsa?*
Anna, the Mayor's daughter.	*Anna, filia magistri civium.*
What remarkable taste!	*egregium spectatorem formarum!*
But she has sparkling eyes and gleaming white rows of teeth.	*at vigent oculi eius nitetque utrimque dentium series.*
He is the spitting image of his father.	*plane patrem reddit et refert.*
He has deep-set eyes.	*oculis est refugis.*

He has freckles and bad teeth.	*ore est sparso et dentibus putrĭdis.*
He is knock-kneed.	*crura sunt vara* (hence the name *Varus!*)
He is bow-legged.	*valgus est.*
Perhaps his unfortunate exterior is balanced by a considerable fortune.	*fortasse formae infelicitas compensatur magnis facultatibus?*
Not at all. He's already bankrupt.	*immo iam decoxit.*
He looks pretty gloomy.	*admodum tristis videtur esse.*
He looks very serious.	*magna est in vultu severitas.*

The Neighbours	**de vicinis**
That's the woman.	*ea est.*
What's her name?	*quod est nomen feminae?*
She is the widow of a man called Textor.	*viduata est morte Textoris cuiusdam.*
She has no end of trouble.	*rerum suarum satis agit* (*sat agit – Ter. Haut.* 2, *1*, *13*).
Her husband, a dissolute and lazy fellow, died several years ago leaving his wife nothing but a host of children.	*marītus ante complures annos decessit, homo dissolutus et ignavus, qui nihil uxori relīquit praeter liberorum gregem.*
She moved here from Leeds three years ago.	*abhinc triennium Ledesia huc commigravit.*
She's better off now.	*nunc eius res meliore loco sunt.*
Who is her father?	*pater quis est?*
He is a respected lawyer, director of a commercial concern and lives in great style.	*iurisconsultus est clari nominis, qui praeest societati mercatorum, homo rei splendidae.*

What's his name? Tell me his first name too. — *quo nomine? adde praenomen!*

Do you know him? — *eumne novisti?*

He's generally considered to be very comfortably off. — *omnes eum in lauta re esse putant.*

Her husband, a dissolute and lazy fellow, died several years ago leaving his wife nothing but a host of children.

He is inordinately rich. — *divitiis abundat.*

He has enough to live on comfortably. — *est, unde commode vivat.*

Those people live well. — *laute vivunt illi* (not *bene!*).

Is her mother still alive? — *vivitne mater?*

Yes. — *vivit.*

Would you tell me the name of the other woman too? — *licetne scire alterius quoque nomen?*

With pleasure. — *maxime!*

In debt	**de aere alieno**
Who is the young man looking at us?	*quisnam hic est adulescens, qui intuetur nos?*
Do you know him?	*tūne novisti eum?*
I know him well and have often seen him.	*bene novi et vidi saepe.*
To the best of my knowledge I've never seen him before today.	*non ĕdĕpol ego eum, quod sciam, unquam ante hunc diem vidi.*
I don't know who the man is nor have I ever set eyes on him before today.	*ego, quis sit homo, nescio neque oculis ante hunc diem unquam vidi.*
But I recognised him straightaway.	*at ego ilico cognovi.*
What's he called?	*quod nomen illi est?*
Charles Miller.	*Carŏlo (-us) Molinario (-us).*
He owes me a hundred pounds.	*libras centum mihi debet.*
You lent him money?	*tu ei credidisti?*
He and I are on reasonably friendly terms.	*intercedit mihi cum eo nonnihil amicitiae.*
He begged me to lend him a hundred pounds (sc. free of interest).	*oravit, ut libras centum sib darem mutuas.*
He pays interest on the money which he borrows.	*pecuniam sumit fenore.*
He is squandering his patrimony.	*conficit patria bona.*
He is incurring debts, has debts.	*aes alienum facit, habet.*
He is deeply in debt.	*in aere alieno est.* *aere alieno demersus est.*
He is up to his eyes in debt.	*animam debet (Ter. Phorm. 4, 3, 56* following the Greek ψυχὴν ὀφείλειν).
He has less than nothing.	*illi minus nihilo est.*
He is in financial difficulty.	*labōrat de pecunia.*

He is no longer very creditworthy.	*fides eum deficere coepit* (*Cic. Font. 34*).
He is bankrupt (see also p. 44).	*a mensa surrexit* or *foro cessit.*
He lives in poverty.	*in egestate est.*
He just manages to keep body and soul together.	*vitam inŏpem sustentat.*
He'll never make his fortune.	*nunquam rem faciet.*
That's life!	*haec est rerum humanarum condicio!*
Why do you worry about other people's problems?	*quid aliena curas?*
Why do you concern yourself with things that have nothing to do with you?	*quid ea curas, quae nihil ad te attinent?*

He is dead — de mortuo

N. has died.	*N.* (*vita*) *decessit.* *N. mortem obiit.*
He took his own life.	*mortem sibi conscivit.* *se ipse vita privavit.*
He committed suicide.	*manus sibi attulit.* *vim sibi intulit.*
Really?	*bona verba!*
No, in fact he died of a disease.	*immo vero morbo confectus est.*
He froze to death.	*frigŏre confectus est.*
He died after a long illness.	*aegrotationibus confectus mortem obiit.*
When will he be buried?	*quando efferetur?*
When will the cremation be?	*quando cremabitur?*
We should like to attend the funeral in order to pay our last respects.	*nos eius funus exsequemur, ut iusta ei faciamus.*

Waiting	**de praestolatione**
Meanwhile I'll wait here for my wife.	*hic ego uxorem interea opperiar.*
I'll wait here for you in front of the door.	*ego vos hic opperiar ante ianuam.*
I have to wait for my brother.	*frater mihi est exspectandus.*
Wait a few moments for me.	*parumper opperire me!*
I'll be back immediately.	*continuo hic adsum!*
Please do so.	*ita quaeso!*
Here I am.	*ecce me!*
Where is Charles? He is nowhere to be seen. Where on earth has he got to?	*ubi Carŏlus? nusquam apparet! quonam ille abiit?*
Here he is.	*ĕccum!*
Here's Charles.	*ĕccum Carŏlum!*
Look! Here he is.	*ĕccum, adest!*
Look! she's over there.	*ĕccillam video!*
Just you wait! (threatening).	*hoc non impune feres!*

Costs	**de impēnsis**
This has cost me a great deal of effort (time).	*plurimum eam in rem operae insumpsi* (*temporis permultum*).
It involved much burning of midnight oil.	*multum lucubrationis impendi.*
This business is costing me a lot of money.	*haec res mihi constat pecunia magna.*
It's costing me an incredible amount.	*pluris mihi constat, quam credas* (*vel credideris*).
For how much a month does he let that flat?	*quanti istud domicilium in singulos menses locat?*
For 17 pounds sterling, 220	*septenis denis libris Anglicis,*

DM, 250 francs.	*ducenis vicenis marcis Germanicis, ducenis quingenis nummis Francogallicis.*
Phew! That's too expensive.	*hui, nimio locat!*
No it's not; many flats nowadays are far more expensive.	*immo multo pluris domicilia pleraque locantur hodie.*
I wouldn't pay so much rent for it.	*ego tanti non conducam.*
How much do you pay for your flat?	*quanti tu habitas?*
As much as the landlord asks, but it's a much better flat.	*tantīdem, quantum ille petit, at multo melius.*
How much do these books cost?	*libros istos quanti vendis?*
Two pounds each.	*binis libris.*
That's too much.	*nimio.*
No, it's very cheap.	*immo minimo.*
How much does he want for this little book?	*quanti hunc libellum indĭcat?*
£1.80.	*una libra et octoginta nummis.*
Tut, tut. As much as that?	*hui, tanti?*
That's a mistake by my assistant; it costs £1.50.	*erravit famulus meus; una libra et quinquaginta nummis constat.*
Have you any change on you?	*aesne habes?*
Yes, both large and small.	*habeo nummos omnis nŏtae.*
I haven't got a single coin in my purse.	*non est (mihi) nummus in crumīna (vel marsuppio).*
I've got some notes on me.	*chartas habeo nummarias mecum.*
Could you lend me a pound until tomorrow?	*potes-ne nunc mutuam libram mihi unam dare, quam cras reddam tibi?*
Here's the money.	*cape hanc pecuniam.*
Take it.	*accipe!*
Do take it.	*quin accipis?*
Where did you get it?	*unde habes?*

Earned by the sweat of my brow.	*labore merui.*
I won it with a Premium Bond.	*sortium beneficio accepi.*

Writing	**de scriptura**
You have attractive handwriting.	*scite scribis manu tua.*
I don't like your handwriting.	*manus tua mihi non placet.*
Your writing is poor.	*parum decōre scribis.* *parum commŏde scribis.*
Your writing is too cramped.	*presse et anguste scribis.*
What sort of paper is this?	*quae charta haec est?*
The paper is somewhat damp and porous.	*charta subumĭda est et transmittit atramentum.*
Do you prefer to write with a hard or soft nib?	*utrum amas scribere calamo* (Late Latin: *penna*) *duriore an molliore?*
Usually I prefer a soft one.	*ego molliore soleo.*
I should like someone to give me a pen-nib.	*alicunde pennam ferream rogabo.*
Take dictation.	*scribitote, quod dicam!*
I can't keep up.	*non possum vocem tuam scribendo assequi!*
You must use shorthand.	*per nŏtas scribendum est!*
A shorthand writer.	*notarius* (*Auson. Ep. 146*).
There's a slip of the pen here.	*hoc mendum est* (*scripturae*)*!*
I've made a mistake.	*in scribendo lapsus sum.*
Be sure you don't cross anything out.	*cave quicquam inducas!*
What are you writing?	*quid scribis?*
I've only made an entry in my notebook.	*in commentariolum meum aliquid rettuli, nihil amplius.*
The handwriting corresponds exactly with your own.	*litterarum figurae* (*vel ductus*) *plane congruunt cum tuis.*

You write it with a 't'.	*scribe hoc per t!*
Black ink. Red ink. Blue ink.	*atramentum. rubramentum. caeruleamentum.*
An inkwell.	*atramentarium.*
An inkblot.	*atramenti macula.*
How much have you written?	*quantum scriptum est?*
A fountain pen with a gold nib.	*graphium atramento repletum (vel atramentarium) acumine aureo praeditum.*
Blotting paper.	*charta bibula.*
A penknife.	*radula chalybeia.*
An india-rubber.	*quadra (vel quadrilla) cummis deletĭlis.*
A ball-point pen.	*graphium pilula armatum (vel stilus sphaera instructus).*
A pencil.	*lapis scriptorius (vel plumbum vel haematītes, ae f.).*
To sharpen.	*cuspidare (vel acuere vel acuminare).*
A pencil-sharpener.	*machinula haematitis cuspidandis vel instrumentum cuspidarium.*
An electric typewriter.	*machina scriptoria (vel dactylographica) electrica vi acta.*
A portable typewriter.	*machinula scriptoria.*
A carbon copy.	*exemplar transscriptum.*
Carbon paper.	*charta transscripticia (vel carbonea).*
A typewriter ribbon.	*taenia colorata.*
A letter file.	*integumentum astrictorium.*
A punch.	*chartarum perforaculum.*
An envelope.	*involŭcrum.*
Paper clips.	*fibiculae metallicae.*
An exercise book.	*chartularum fasciculus.*
A stapler.	*chartarum consutorium.*
A wastepaper-basket.	*s(c)irpiculus chartarum.*

A stationer.	*chartarius.*
A stationery shop.	*taberna chartaria.*
An address book.	*liber civium index.*
A briefcase.	*theca scriptoria (vel libraria).*
A printing-press.	*officina libraria. typographēum.*

At Home. Not at Home — **domi, non domi**

Where are you off to, dear Leonard?	*quo noster Leonardus?*
I was on my way to you.	*ad te ibam.*
Where are you going to take me?	*quo me duces?*
Where? To my place of course.	*quo ego te? ad me scilicet!*
My brother has been waiting for you for ages.	*te iam dudum exspectat frater meus.*
Has he come back from his journey?	*rediitne ex itinere?*
Where is he then?	*ubĭnam est?*
At my house.	*apud me domi.*
Unfortunately he has gone already.	*abit, antequam vellem!*
He is not at home.	*fŏris est.*
He has already made off.	*iam se amovit.*
I'm going back home.	*domum me recipio (vel me confero, revertor, repeto).*
Why are you going there?	*quid illuc? – quid eo?*
I want to see what's going on at home.	*visam, quid domi agatur.*
As you were away I took a friend with me.	*adduxi amicum te absente.*
Do you know who I ran into?	*scisne, in quem inciderim?*
My dear friend Leonard.	*in Leonardum, hominem mihi amicissimum!*

May I make a suggestion for this evening? — *licetne in vesperum hodiernum vobis aliquid commendare?*

Yes, please. — *licet.*

Let's go to the pictures. — *cinematographēum adeamus!*

We'll see a splendid film. — *magnificam imaginum videbimus seriem.*

Then we'll go to a night club and make eyes at a luscious dancing girl . . .

Then we'll go to a night club and make eyes at a luscious dancing girl. — *deinde in cauponam nocturnam intrabimus atque saltatrīcem admirabimur bellam.*

Will she do a striptease too? — *etiamne in saltando veste deposita corporis formam proponet?*

You're asking too much. — *nimium postulas.*

A talkie.	*pellicŭla (cinematographica) sonans.*

Getting up	**de surrectione**
Is it time to get up?	*estne tempus, ut surgamus?*
Yes, it's high time.	*est tempus maximum.*
Are you still in bed?	*in lecto etiamnunc es?*
Certainly.	*ita.*
Is Henry still asleep?	*Henrīcus dormitne adhuc?*
Yes.	*dormit.*
How very like him (cf. p. 23).	*hoc isto dignum.* *non alienum est ab eius moribus.*
Get up and wake him.	*surge, ut eum excĭtes!*
Hallo there, you good-for-nothing, I've been shouting myself hoarse for ages, and you won't wake up.	*heus, heus, furcifer* (*vel homo nequissime*), *iamdūdum irraucēsco clamore nec tu tamen expergiscĕris!*
Get up quickly or I'll shake you out of your sleep.	*aut ocius surge aut ego tibi somnum istum excutiam!*
When will you have slept off yesterday's drunkenness?	*quando crāpŭlam hesternam edormiveris?*
Aren't you ashamed to go on snoring in broad daylight?	*nonne te pudet in multam lucem stertĕre?*
While he's stretching himself and yawning, a whole hour goes by.	*dum distendit nervos, dum oscĭtat, tota abit hora.*
When did you get up?	*tu quando surrexisti e lecto?*
I got up early.	*ego mane surrexi.*
I usually get up before dawn.	*equidem soleo ante lucem surgere.*
It is hardly light yet.	*vixdum diluxit.*
It is still completely dark.	*adhuc multa nox est.*
Put the light on.	*accende lucernam!*

Hurry up! You should have finished that by now.	*move te ocius: iam haec te fecisse oportuit!*
I can't do two things at once.	*non possum simul sorbēre et flare* (*Plaut. Most. 3, 2. 100*).
What's the time?	*quid horae est?*
Five past six.	*post sextam minutae quinque* (see p. 18).
Did you know that it was so late?	*tune sciebas hoc esse tempus?*
No, I didn't know.	*nesciebam.*
Is that so?	*itane?*
Really, I didn't know.	*nesciebam, inquam.*
Is there some water in the wash-basin?	*estne aqua in trulleo?*
Fetch some water to wash one's hands and face.	*affer aquam ad lavandas manus et faciem!*
Bring me some water to wash my hands; they are dirty.	*affer aquam manibus; manus meae sordidae sunt.*
Hurry up! Get a move on!	*propĕra! quid cessas?*
Have you got soap and a clean towel?	*habesne saponem et mantēle recens?*
Toothbrush, toothpaste, mouthwash.	*pēnĭculus* (*vel pēnicillus*), *dentifricium, aqua dentibus purgandis.*
A razor.	*novacŭla* (*vel tonsorius culter, -tri*).
A safety razor.	*novacŭla machinālis.*
A razor-blade.	*lamella rasoria.*
An electric razor.	*novacŭla vi electrica acta* (*novacŭla electrica*).
I must go to the loo first.	*antea alvum exoneratum ibo.*
Have you washed already?	*lavistine iam?*
I haven't dried myself yet.	*nondŭm me tersi.*
I'll go and have a bathe today.	*lavatum hodie ibo.*

Morning Preparations	**de matutina corporis curatione (vel cultu)**
Have you combed and brushed your hair?	*pexistine capillos et composuisti?*
Yes.	*ita.*
Put on a clean shirt.	*muta interŭlam* (*scil. tunicam*)*!*

Your trousers are in the wardrobe

Have you polished your boots?	*repurgataene sunt călĭgae?*
My shoes are clean.	*calcei sunt extersi.*
Your hat and clothes must be thoroughly brushed.	*pileus et vestimenta pēniculo detergenda sunt.*
Where are my shoes?	*calceamenta ubi sunt?*
Your trousers are in the wardrobe.	*brācae* (hence breeches) *in armario sunt.*
I've got my shoes on now.	*iam calceatus sum.*

Are you ready at last?	*tandemne paratus es?*
You see how badly dressed I am.	*vides, quam sim pannosus!* (lit: ragged).
I'm often ashamed to go out when I see how smart other people are.	*saepe me taedet prodire in publicum, cum video, quam culti sint alii.*
And I could do with a fur coat.	*vestis pellīta quoque mihi deest.*
The bed has to be made.	*lecti stragula componenda est.*
Let's have breakfast now.	*iam sumamus ientāculum.*
You're right; it's time for breakfast.	*recte mones; ientemus!*

In the Study	**in umbrāculo**
He is a most industrious student.	*summo studio in litteris versatur.*
You lead the life of a snail.	*tu mihi vidēris coclĕae (cochlĕae) vitam agere.*
In what way?	*qui sic?*
Because you spend all your time lurking in the house and never crawl out of it.	*quia perpetuo domi lătĭtas nec unquam prorēpis.*
You'll rust away at home.	*tu domi sĭtum* (mould, rust) *duces.*
I have a job to do at home; outside there's nothing to occupy me.	*est, quod agam domi; fŏris nihil est negotii.*
You're too attached to your books.	*nimium affixus es libris.*
Do give yourself a little break, I beg you.	*quaeso tandem aliquantulum tibi parce!*
You're wearing yourself to a shred with all this study.	*immodico studio ipse te macĕras.*
I live for my books, and I would die for my books.	*mihi vero vel immŏri chartis dulce est.*

'Live for' is all right, but I don't think much of the 'die for'.	*equidem 'immorari' probo, 'immŏri' non probo.*
In such good company I never suffer from boredom.	*talis sodalicii nunquam me capit taedium.*
One never has enough of one's work.	*non est studiorum satietas.*
That's true, but there's a limit in all things.	*ita est, sed tamen est modus quidam.*
The rarer the pleasure, the greater the enjoyment.	*'voluptates commendat rarior usus' (Juv. 11, 208).*
Night and day you're at your books.	*studiis vacas noctes ac dies.*
What are you up to now?	*quid agis nunc?*
I'm free at the moment.	*equidem otium ago.*
Better to be disengaged than ineffective.	*praestat otiosum esse quam nihil agere (Plin. Ep. 1, 9, 8).*
Perhaps I am disturbing you while you're engaged on some serious business?	*ego te fortasse occupatum seriis negotiis interpello?*
No, I have nothing to do. I was beginning to feel bored.	*immo maxime vacuum. iam me ceperat otii taedium.*
Forgive me if I have interrupted you at an inconvenient time.	*da veniam, si te parum opportuno tempore interpellavi.*
No, you've come just at the right time.	*immo in tempore advĕnis.*
You've arrived just when I wanted you.	*optatus ades.*
No, you've come at a good moment.	*immo opportune te huc attulisti.*
How long have you been a student?	*quamdiu iam litteris operam dedisti?*
A student.	*civis academicus.*
Students.	*iuvenes litterarum.*
In what subjects are you specialising?	*cui potissimum studiorum generi te addīcis?*
In medicine? Or law? Or theology? In classical or modern	*utrum medicinae? an iuris prudentiae? an theologĭae? an*

languages? In philosophy? In physical education?	*linguis antiquis an recentioribus? philosophĭae? arti exercitatoriae?*
I have not committed myself to one particular subject.	*nondum ulli me plane addixi.*
What profession do you intend to follow?	*quodnam vitae genus amplectēris?*
I don't yet know which I am fit for.	*nondum video, cui sim accommodatus.*
All over the world medicine is the surest way of earning one's living.	*medicina ubĭvis terrarum certissimum est viaticum.*
Law leads on to political theory.	*iuris prudentia viam aperit ad rei publicae doctrinam.*
Theology would appeal to me particularly if the constant wranglings of the theologians did not put me off.	*theologĭa mihi imprimis placeret, nisi nimiae theologorum contentiones me offenderent.*
In philosophy I'm an eclectic.	*in philosophĭa e multis summam concipio.*
The University.	*universitas litterarum* (*vel studiorum*).
The Technical University.	*technica studiorum universitas.*
The Veterinary College.	*veterinaria studiorum universitas.*
He is a corresponding Fellow of the British School at Athens.	*socius est ab epistulis Archaeologici Instituti Britannici Athenis collocati.*
The Royal Society.	*Regalis Societas pro scientia naturali promovenda.*
The Students' Union.	*studiosorum iuvenum consociatio.*
An academic ceremony.	*sollemne academicum.*

The veterinary college

Radio and Television — de re radiophonica et (radio) televisifica

(cf. Vita Latina No. 22–24, 1964/65: De Germaniae quadragenaria re radiophonica = Forty Years of Broadcasting in Germany by C. Eichenseer.)

Shall we go to a concert this evening?	*audiemusne hodie vesperi concentum (vel certamen musicum) in Odēo?*
A famous orchestra is playing.	*symphoniăci incluti canent.*
An excellent singer (f) will be accompanied by an orchestra.	*cantatrix egregia ad symphoniam canet.*
The orchestra is playing chamber-music.	*symphoniaci fidibus canunt.*
The conductor.	*concentus ductor.*
I prefer to stay at home and listen to the Barber of Seville on the radio.	*mālo domi radiophonice audire Tonsorem Hispalensem.*

But the radio is no substitute for a live concert.	*transmissio radiophonica non idem valet quod verus concentus vocum, nervorum, tibiarum.*
You are right, but I do like listening to Rome.	*recte tu quidem. nihilominus placet audire symphonĭam Romanam.*
To Rome?	*heus tu, quid dicis?*
I mean to the concerts in the Mausoleum of Augustus.	*symphonĭas dico illius praeclarissimi Odēi, quod est Romae in Mausolēo imperatoris Augusti.*
Radio London takes great pains to keep up to date.	*statio Londonienis sedulo recentissima offert.*
Broadcasting.	*radiotelephonĭa.*
To switch on the radio.	*radiophōnum expedire* (*vel excitare*).
To switch off the radio.	*radiophōnum sistere.*
The radio set.	*instrumentum radiophonicum.*
Short-, Medium-, Long-Wave, Ultra-short wave.	*undae* (*radiophonicae*) *breves, mediae, longae, supérbrĕves.*
The amplifying valve.	*lampas amplificatrix.*
The wavelength.	*undulationis longitudo.*
The loudspeaker.	*mega*(*lo*)*phōnum.*
The wall-socket.	*capsella contactus* (*electrici*).
The battery.	*pīla electrica.*
The switch.	*epitonium electricum.*
The transmitting station.	*statio transmissoria* (*vel emissoria*).
The broadcast.	*emissio* (*vel transmissio, diffusio*) *radiophonica* (*vel televisifica*).
Interference.	*conturbatio.*
The record player.	*armarium discorum sonantium. discotheca.*
Television.	(*radio*)*televisio.*

The colour television set.	*instrumentum* (*vel scrinium*) (*radio*)*televisorium* [(*radio*)*televisificum*] *quod efficit ordinem imaginum omnibus coloribus pictarum.*
Can you see the programmes clearly with an indoor aerial?	*potesne emissiones televisificas clare videre antemna in conclavi posita?*
No, I have one on the roof.	*immo antemna mea in tecto posita est.*
The daily news bulletins.	*nuntii cottidiani* (*vel cottidie relati, referendi*).

Breakfast and Lunch — de ientaculo et prandio

Breakfast is ready.	*ientaculum paratum est.*
Would you like to have breakfast with us?	*ientabisne tu nobiscum?*
Have you had breakfast yet?	*iamne ientasti?*
When do you usually have breakfast?	*quando soles ientare?*
Do sit down.	*assīde quaeso!*
Will you take tea or coffee?	*sumesne theānam an arabicam potiunculam?*
Coffee, please.	*da quaeso arabicam!*
Here is the cream, and there's the sugar.	*habes hanc crāmam, illud sacchărum.*
Please help yourself.	*velim tu ipse sumas.*
Or would you prefer a cup of chocolate?	*an potionem ex theobrōmăte* (*vel ex faba mexicana*) *confectam mavis?*
Put plenty of sugar in the tea, and add a few slices of lemon.	*condi theam plurimo sacchăro et nonnullis orbiculis* [*māli*] *citrěi.*

Would you like tea with rum?	*placetne thea cum vino Indico?*
How do you like your coffee?	*dic, cuius saporis haec potio cafearia.*
Is it strong enough?	*satisne valida est?*
It's absolutely superb.	*est optima mehercule.*
It's rather weak.	*aliquanto imbecillior est.*
Would you like another cup of coffee?	*sumesne aliquid etiam cafeariae potionis?*
Half a cup please, if you don't mind.	*semiplenum dato (sc. potorium pōcillum), si commodum erit.*
There's nothing here for me to eat.	*hic nihil est, quod edam.*
There's bread.	*est panis.*
Yes, but it's black and coarse.	*est, sed ater et furfurĕus.*
Please may I have a piece of white bread?	*numquid tibi molestum erit dare panis siliginĕi aliquantulum?*
Here are rye-bread, white bread and some rolls.	*habes panem e secăli, e siligine factum, paniculos similaceos.*
If you don't like bread by itself, eat an apple with it, or if you prefer a piece of Swiss cheese.	*si fastīdis panem nullo addito obsonio, sumito malum vel, si males, casĕi Alpini aliquantulum.*
Here's the butter.	*butȳrum (vel butūr) habe.*
Or would you prefer blackcurrant jelly or some jam?	*An mavis iusculum ex acinis ribis nigri concretum vel pomarium liquamen?*
What I like best is bread thickly coated with butter and quince marmalade.	*mihi imprimis placet panis butȳro et malis Cydoniis gelatis bene unctus.*
Here are three kinds of eggs for you: boiled, fried and scrambled eggs.	*habete triplex ovorum genus: elixa, assa, rudiculā peragitata (commixta, versata).*
They are all quite fresh, not more than two days old.	*omnia sunt recentissima, intra biduum nata.*
Do you prefer your eggs hard or soft boiled?	*visne concreta sint an fluida ova?*

Please may I have a hard-boiled egg?	*da queso concretum ovum.*
Would you like a slice of ham or roast beef?	*visne de perna vel bubula tosta?*
A small piece of smoked ham if it's not too much trouble.	*paululum fumosae pernae dato, nisi molestum erit* or *da quaeso aliquantulum.*
Bacon doesn't agree with me.	*lardi esum non fero.*
Lunch.	*prandium.*
Let's have lunch.	*prandeamus.*
I'm hungry, thirsty.	*esŭrio, sĭtio.*
My stomach's rumbling.	*vacuus mihi venter crepĭtat.*
For various reasons I should prefer a soused herring today.	*certis de causis hodie mālo aringum acēto perfusum.*
Have you some hot sausages?	*habesne tŏmācŭla ferventia?* (*Petron. 31, 11*).
A dozen oysters, please.	*peto duodecim ostrĕas.*
A tasty stew.	*gustum delicatum.*
Would you like a beefsteak?	*visne de carne bubŭla frustum assum?*
Yes, if there's some Worcester Sauce to go with it.	*peto, si gărum praesto est.* (But note that *garum* was made from fish.)
You'll have to make do with a small helping.	*boni* (*gen. pretii*) *consulite haec pauca.*
Help yourselves to eggs and lettuce.	*admovete manus ovis et lactūcis!*
Have you still got room for a piece of Boeuf en Croûte?	*libetne bubulae gausăpātae aliquid etiam sumere?*

NB: *gausapātus:* literally wrapped in a frieze (*gausăpa*).

No, thank you; I've had plenty.	*benigne; iam satis est.*
What would you like to drink?	*quid cupis tibi dari potandum?*

First an apéritif, then grapejuice or applejuice.	*primum prŏpŏma (Pall. 3, 32;* Greek πρόπομα), *deinde sucum ex uvis vel malis expressum.*

An Invitation to Dinner	**ad cenam voco**
Dinner (the main meal).	*cena.*
Are you dining at home today?	*cenabis hodie domi?*
No, I'm dining out.	*foris cenaturus sum.*
May I ask at whose house?	*cĕdo apud quem?*
At my father-in-law's, mother-in-law's.	*apud socĕrum meum, socrum meam.*
In that case I invite you to dinner tomorrow.	*in crastĭnum igitur te ad cenam voco.*
I beg you to dine with me tomorrow.	*cras ut mecum cenes oro.*
Thank you; but I'm afraid that it won't be possible.	*ago gratias; at vereor, ne non liceat.*
I'm afraid that I can't.	*ut possim, metuo.*
I'll come if it's at all possible.	*veniam, si modo licebit.*
Why won't it be possible?	*cur non licebit?*
How come? For what reason?	*quid ita? quam ob rem?*
On what grounds?	*quid causae?*
What is there to stop you?	*quid obstiterit, quominus possis?*
I have to stay at home.	*domi mihi manendum est.*
It's essential for me to stay at home.	*necesse est mihi domi manere.*
I'm expecting some guests myself on that day.	*aliquot ipse eo die convivas opperior.*
A few good friends intend to dine with us that evening.	*aliquot amiculi constituēre ea vespera domi nostrae cenare.*
Otherwise I should love to come.	*aliōqui libens venirem.*

I can't come now with the best will in the world. — *nunc, ut maxime cupiam, non possum.*

But at least you must come to dinner on the day after tomorrow; that's this Thursday. — *saltem perendĭno die ad cenam venias necesse est, die Iovis proximo.*

Lavish hospitality may be welcome at the time, but it leads to a headache and an upset stomach on the next day . . .

I can't promise. — *non possum polliceri.*

I can't accept definitely. — *affirmare istud tibi non possum.*

I can't give a firm undertaking. — *promittere certum nequeo.*

I'll come as soon as we can find a date that suits us both. — *veniam, ubi utrique nostrum videbitur commodissimum.*

I accept your invitation with thanks. — *libenter me venturum promitto.*

But please don't go to any special trouble. — *at cave quicquam paraveris praeter cottidiana.*

Lavish hospitality may be welcome at the time, but it leads to a headache and an upset stomach on the next day. — *qui prolixe fuerit acceptus, eo die fortasse suaviter afficietur, sed postridie dolebit caput, crūdus erit stŏmăchus.*

You won't have even a hint of an upset stomach on the day after. — *tu postridie nullam cruditatem senties.*

At Table — **cenemus!**

The table is being laid. — *linteo iam insternitur mensa.*

Dinner is ready. — *cena parata est.*

Let's sit down. — *discumbamus.*

I don't want to allocate seats; let everybody sit where they like. — *ego nulli designabo locum; sumat sibi, quem quisque volet.*

Here's a comfortable seat for someone who likes the fire. — *qui delectatur igni, hic commodius accumbet.*

Here's a comfortable seat for someone who likes a view. — *quem delectat prospectus, hic sedeat.*

Would you like to sit here on the right side of the table? — *tu quaeso dextrum hoc latus mensae occŭpa.*

I'll take the seat in the corner here. — *ego hunc angulum capiam.*

We can't allow that; you should be at the head of the table. — *non patiemur; primus tibi debetur locus.*

Come, we've delayed long enough. Sit down, please. — *agite, satis morarum. accumbite, quaeso.*

Now's the time to see to our physical well-being. — *vivamus nunc curemusque cŭtem (vel cŭticŭlam).*

Let's enjoy ourselves. — *indulgebimus geniis. (sc. nostris).*

Begone dull care! — *valeant curae!*

Please would you say grace? — *deum, quaeso, invŏca!*

Start serving. — *appōne epulas!*

Bon appétit! — *sit felix convivium!* / *bene sit universo coetui!*

But why have you gone to so much trouble? — *sed quid tantus apparatus?*

Better too much than too little!	*praestat aliquid superesse quam deesse.*
But that's contrary to our agreement.	*haud ita convenerat!*

The Soup — de sorbitione

Would you like some soup?	*placetne sumere sorbitionem?*
I'd love some.	*amabo.*
No thank you; I'm not particularly keen on soup.	*benigne; haud ita grata mihi est.*
The soup is excellent.	*haec sorbitio omni laude digna!*
I simply must congratulate you.	*non possum, quin maximopere te laudem.*
Glad you like it.	*gaudeo te ea delectari.*
You're going to so much trouble on my account.	*tu multum laboris mea causa capis!*
Behave just as you would at home.	*proinde agito, ac si domi sis tuae!*
I've every intention of doing so.	*istud iam plane mihi persuasi.*

The Wine — de vino

I've become rather thirsty.	*contraxi* (*vel collegi*) *aliquid sĭtis.*
Do you prefer red or white wine?	*utrum mavis, rubrum an candidum?*
I like both equally.	*equidem utroque iuxta delector.*
The colour is unimportant if the taste is good.	*parvi interest, quo sit colore,* (*dum*)*modo săpor placeat.* *parvi interest, quem habeat colorem, si săpiat bene.*

I should like to hear your verdict as you're an expert. *iudicium tuum audire cupio, hominis harum rerum peritissimi.*

This Moselle of yours scores high marks; it seems a noble wine. *istud vinum Mosellanum notae est bonae, generosum videtur esse.*

The colour is unimportant if the taste is good.

It's a 1959 Berncastel Doctor. *est Alberonis Castelli Doctor anni MCMLIX.*

My wife prefers the red Burgundy because it's more mellow and agrees with her better. *uxor mea rubrum vinum Burgundinum praefert, quod lenius (vel mitius) et salubrius sit.*

Have you a corkscrew? *habesne tormentum cochlĕātum extrācŭlŭm (cochlĕa* snail)*?*

Open the bottle. *relĭne lagōnam!*

I've opened it. *relēvi eam.*

Punches: (a) the bowl; (b) the wine.	(*a*) *crātēr*(*a*); (*b*) *arōmatītes* (*-ae*) *m.* (ἀρωματίτης = aromatic wine).
This year's new wine.	*mustum hornum* (= *huius anni*).
Over a glass of wine.	*in vino.*
As we sat over our wine.	*per vinum.*

Poultry, Roasts, Dessert — de altilibus, assis, bellariis

Let's start carving this capon.	*quid cunctamur cāpum* (*vel cāpōnem*) *hunc discerpere?*
Would you prefer a wing or a leg?	*utrum mavis de ala an de poplitibus?*
Whichever you wish. I have no preference.	*utrum vis, mea nihil refert.*
With this sort of bird the wings are regarded as the best part; in others the legs are generally thought to be more tasty.	*in hoc genere alis primae partes tribuuntur; in ceteris poplĭtes lautiores putat vulgus.*
This meal is easily digestible.	*hic cibus facillimus est ad concoquendum.*
Prepared in this way the food tastes good.	*hoc modo coctus placet cibus.*
I'm delighted that you were satisfied with the first course.	*quod primo fuisti ferculo contentus, valde gaudeo.*
Would you rather have veal or lamb?	*utrum de vitulīnis an de ovillis carnibus mavis?*
I prefer beef.	*būbŭlis* (*sc. carnibus*) *magis delector.*
I'm remarkably fond of pork.	*suillas carnes mirum in modum amo.*
The sauce is really delicious.	*ius est iucundissimum.*
Let everybody help themselves to what they fancy.	*sumat sibi quisque, quod gratum est animo.*

Here comes the main dish of our modest meal; it's a shoulder of mutton, but first-rate quality.	*videtis huius cenulae summam (vel pompam, Martial 10, 31, 4); armus est ovillus, sed exquisitus.*
Would you like some leg of this hare?	*vis de his leporīnis clunibus?*
Or would you rather have a piece of back?	*an de tergo mavis?*
Do you like roast goose?	*delectantne te anserīnae carnes?*
Yes, I like it very much.	*non mediocriter me iuvant.*
Would you like some goose-liver? It was already regarded as a delicacy by the ancients.	*libetne de iecŏre anserino, quod apud veteres in deliciis cumprimis habebatur?*
Goose fat.	*ădeps (gen. adĭpis) anserīnus (vel -a) (Pliny).*
Would anyone like more of anything?	*libetne cuiquam quicquam amplius?*
Nothing at all.	*nihil omnino.*
That was a three course meal you served.	*cenam tribus fercŭlis praebuisti (Suet. Aug. 74).*
Lastly the dessert.	*ad extremum mensa secunda (vel ĕpidīpnis, idis f. Petron, Mart., ἐπιδειπνίς).*
Take the plates away, and bring small ones.	*tolle cătīnos, affer catillos!*
Take my knife away; it has fallen on the floor.	*tolle cultrum meum, qui humi decĭdit.*
Here are cheese and butter, and over there is the fruit: nuts, melons, roast chestnuts, yellow plums, stewed pears and peaches.	*hic caseus būtȳrumque, illic fruges: nuces, melōnes (vel pepŏnes), castănĕae tostae, pruna cērĕa, condīta pira, persica.*
If we've had enough, we'll go into the garden.	*placato stomacho ibimus in hortum.*
I hope you enjoyed the meal.	*bene sit tibi! sit saluti! bene tibi vertat (sc. cena)!*

Have a cigarette.	*ēn papȳrus fumifĕra* (*vel nicotiānum bacillum, tabāci bacillum*).

A Walk	**de ambulatione**
It would be better to get up from our chairs and go for a walk.	*quin potius e sellis surgamus ambulaturi.*
Let's take the ladies with us.	*ducamus nobiscum fēmĭnās.*
A short walk will give us an appetite.	*mem efficiet* (*vel acuet stomachum*) *ambulatiuncula.*
Let's go then.	*age, eamus ergo!*
Yes.	*eamus!*
Go over there.	*i!*

He has taken a trip into the country!

Off you go.	*abi!*
Let's get a move on.	*festinemus nonnihil!*
You go in front.	*antecede! (vel i prae!)*
Suits me.	*ego vero libens!*
You accompany me.	*sequere me!*
Right. I'll accompany you.	*age, te sequor.*
Well I'll catch you up shortly.	*age, paulo post veniam.*
He has gone for a walk.	*abiit deambulatum.*
A walk? Where to?	*deambulatum? quo?*
He has taken a trip into the country.	*rus excucurrit.*
On foot?	*pedibusne? (plur.!)*
No, by car.	*immo automatariā raedā (vel autoraeda).*
By tram.	*transviaria raeda.*
He has gone ahead by a short-cut.	*alia via compendiaria antevertit.*
With everything full of the joys of spring I'm amazed that there are people who like the smoke and soot of the city.	*nunc, cum omnia vernent et rideant, demiror esse, qui urbe fumosa delectentur.*
There's a panorama here.	*prospectus hic late patet!*
As the sun sets there's a wonderful view over the river.	*supremo sole amnis aspectus oculos mirum in modum iuvat.*
Here there's a view over the mountains.	*hinc prospectus est ad montes.*
I can see vineyards.	*vitifĕros colles (vel vineas) video.*
Where are they?	*ubĭnam?*
In the valley in front of us. Do you see them?	*in hac valle obvia. videsne?*
I can't pick them out; I'm too short-sighted.	*illos discernere non possum; parum prospiciunt oculi mei.*
They're too far away for me to recognise them.	*intervallum longius est, quam ut eos cognoscam.*

Here are some binoculars for you.	*en tibi telescopium!*
How beautiful the colour of the flowers is!	*quam blandus florum color!*
Now you could choose another pleasant spot.	*superest, ut locum elĭgas amoenum.*
Yes, I'll show you a place that combines shady woodland, green meadows and bubbling springs.	*ego vero tibi locum ostendam, ubi nec nemŏris umbram nec pratorum viriditatem nec fontium scatĕbras desideres.*
The walk has tired me.	*fessus sum de via.*
Is there an inn in this village?	*estne in hoc vico deversorium publicum?*

An Encounter	**de congressu**
Where do you come from? Where are you going?	*unde vĕnis? – quo tendis?*
Where are you off to?	*quo tu nunc abis?*
Where are you hurrying?	*quo nunc properas?*
Where are you going in such a hurry?	*quo tu tam celeri gradu tendis?*
Where are you making for?	*quonam te confers?*
Where are you heading?	*quo nunc iter est?*
What way will you go?	*quanam iturus es?* / *qua ibis?*
Here. There. Through the market. Here to the left.	*hac. illac. per fŏrum. hac ad sinistram.*
All right. I'll come along with you.	*comitabor igitur te.*
I'll join you and escort you to your hotel.	*assectabor et deducam te ad deversorium tuum.*
Don't go a long way round for my sake.	*ne mea causa feceris viae tuae dispendium.*
I've nothing to do and am glad	*nihil habeo, quod agam, nec*

of the exercise provided my company isn't disagreeable to you. — *sum piger, nisi tibi sim molestus comes.*

It's quite a stretch from here. — *hinc longŭle est.*

Where does this road lead? — *haec via quo fert?*

Let's join this road here. — *hanc viam ingrediamur!*

We go straight on. — *recta* (*via*) *pergimus.*

We must cross over there. — *illuc transeundum!*

I'll say farewell here. — *hic te superis commendo.*

You mustn't accompany me any further. — *iam nolo me comiteris.*

In the Café — in thermopōlio

Hallo, Charles! How are you? — *salve, Carŏle! quid agitur?*

Not so bad, and how are things with you? — *contentus sum, et quo loco sunt res tuae?*

So, so. — *varia fortuna.*

Shall we go into this Café and have a cosy chat? — *intremus in hoc thermopolium atque commode colloquamur inter nos!*

What can I get you, gentlemen? — *quid optatis?*

Perhaps an iced drink? — *fortasse nivatam potionem aliquam?*

Bring me an espresso coffee, please. — *apporta, quaeso, potionem arabicam coram expressam!*

Tea with milk and sugar and some pastry for me, please. — *mihi vero theanam potionem saccharo lacteque condītam et crustulorum nonnihil, quaeso.*

The proprietor is an admirable and charming host. — *thermopōla est caupo egregius gratiosusque.*

He takes great trouble over all his customers. — *studiose omnibus praestat hospitibus operam.*

Young girls suck lemonade through straws.
puellae vix adultae pōscas (vel citrĭnas) sugunt stipŭlis.

On cold winter days I often drink a cup of piping hot chocolate here.
frigidis hiemis diebus hic saepe ex mexicana făba (vel ex theobromate) potionem calidissimam sorbĭlo.

Young girls suck lemonade through straws . . .

The landlord serves excellent beer.
thermopola egregiam divendit cerevesiam.

He also offers delicious sandwiches.
far(c)ta pastilla sapore praebet iucundo.

He stocks a good brandy.
bonam potionem Coniacensem offert.

Many daily newspapers, both British and foreign, and a variety of illustrated periodicals are available to customers.
multa acta diurna, et Britannica et externa, atque varii commentarii imaginibus luce pictis ornati in hospitum sunt potestate.

Waiter, the bill please!
redde, puer, quaeso rationem!

Let me pay, Charles. Another time it will be your turn.
sine, Carole, me persolvere; alias tuae erunt partes.

Very kind of you. I should also like to buy a bar of chocolate for my wife and a few sweets for the children. — *benigne dicis; uxori theobromătis quadras et liberis nonnulla bellaria emam.*

What a model father you are! — *o patrem familias exemplarem!*

At the Barber's — **in tonstrina**

What can I do for you? — *quid est, quod cupias?*

I should like my hair cut. — *recīdas, quaeso, capillum meum!*

You'll have to wait a moment. — *paulisper maneas necesse est.*

There's a queue. — *ordo servatur.*

Please would you give me a periodical? — *id amabo, praebe mihi aliquem libellum periodicum!*

It's your turn. — *ordo te vocat.*

How would you like your hair cut? — *quemadmodum cupis capillum detondēri?*

Short back and sides (literally: temples and back of the head). — *brevis fiat a temporibus et occipitio.*

Would you like your hair washed? — *optasne, ut lavetur capillus?*

May I put a little hair-oil on? — *licetne unguenti paulum crinibus illinere?*

Just enough to make the hair lie properly. — *tantum, ut crines queant comi.*

I should like a shave as well. — *barbam quoque velim novacula radi.*

Shall I rub some after-shave on your face, Eau de Cologne for example? — *osne confrĭcem aqua odorata, velut Agrippinensi?*

Is there anything you would like to take with you? — *ecquid domum vis auferre?*

Please may I have some toilet-soap, shaving-soap and a few razor-blades? — *da mihi, sodes, sāpōnes et lavatorium et rasorium praeterea decem rasorias laminas.*

I need a new shaving-brush. — *novo penicillo rasorio mihi opus est.*

A Fair — de sollemni publico

Come with me. I'll show you a fairground, something quite unique. — *mecum venias! Lŏcŭm celebritatis pŏpŭlāris, rem singularem, tibi monstrabo.*

We enter the narrow streets of a small town consisting of booths, huts and stalls. — *plătēas angustas oppidi tŭgŭriis, casis, tabernis compositi ingredimur.*

This town is movable and can be shifted to another spot; a week ago this spot was desolate and empty, and in a week's time it will be empty again. — *hoc oppidum mobile est et in alium locum transportari potest; ante octo dies haec area fuit vasta et vacua et post octo dies in vacuum redibit.*

But today it is alive with countless people wishing for a few hours to forget their everyday worries. — *hodie autem innumerabiles homines curas cottidianas per paucas horas oblituri ibi versantur.*

Let's join them in walking through these streets. — *nos quoque per has plateas ambulemus!*

There's a charlatan for you! — *ecce circulator!*

Come on in! Come on in! In this booth you'll see something you've never seen before. — *intrate, intrate! In hoc tŭgŭrio aspicietis, quod adhuc nunquam aspexistis.*

What will there be inside? — *quid intus erit?*

Perhaps a human or animal freak. — *fortasse miraculum hominis vel bestiae.*

The world asks to be deceived.	*mundus vult decipi.*
There on the platform outside his tent we see a wrestler with his huge body and powerful limbs; through a trumpet he's inviting us to a wrestling match.	*illo loco in crĕpīdine tabernaculi luctatorem corpore maximo membrisque robustissimis videmus; tuba canens ad luctationis certamen invitat.*
There are other loudmouths shouting their heads off too.	*alii quoque nugatores magna voce clamant.*
There! Can't you hear a confused sound of music?	*euge! Nonne audis sonos musicae perturbatos?*
Over there revolving wooden horses are suspended, and their riders are being carried around in a circle.	*ibi equi lignei pendentes gyrantŭr equisque homines vehuntur, qui in orbe(m) circumaguntur.*
Outside that tent all manner of sweets and confectionery are on sale.	*ante illud tentorium cuppēdiae et dulcedines variae offeruntur.*
Oh! Look over there! There's a swing on which crackling people are being tossed backwards and forwards.	*proh! Illuc specta! Ibi oscillum est, quo homines cachinnantes iactantur.*
Over here there's a wine bar, and over there a beer hall, and everywhere there are people drinking and enjoying themselves.	*hoc loco vini tabernam videmus, illo loco cervēsiae cauponam et ubique homines bibentes et laetantes.*
Although such a festival is intended primarily for the young, mature adults can still spend a happy hour there in memory of their younger days.	*quamquam tale sollemne imprimis ad iuventutis usum aptum est, tamen temperata quoque aetas temporum praeteritorum memor hoc loco libenter per horam quandam exsultat.*

From Tax-office to Bank	**ex sede officii fiscalis ad argentariam mensam**
Poor old me!	*heu me miserum!*
Where have you come from?	*unde venisti?*
From the tax-office.	*a sede officii fiscalis.*
I learned there that I have to pay at once a higher tax on my profits than I had expected.	*ibi maius tributum ex fructibus, quam putaveram, statim mihi esse persolvendum comperi.*
I was fined recently for not paying my income-tax in time.	*equidem nuperrime, quod tributum ex reditibus intra diem certam non solvissem, multatus sum.*
Pay the rest in instalments.	*residuum per partes ratas solve!*
I wasn't allowed to do that.	*id mihi non est concessum.*
I paid by cheque, not in cash.	*non nummis praesentibus, sed pecunia perscripticia solvi.*
I hope the Midland Bank will lend me the rest on security.	*Argentariam Mediterraneam mihi sub pignore pecuniam necessariam credituram esse spero.*
I have shares and bonds deposited there.	*ibi collatae pecuniae syngraphae et nomina publica a me sunt deposita.*
I keep some jewellery in their safe.	*nonnullas quoque gemmas in thesauro argentariae habeo repositas.*
Do you play the Stock Exchange?	*esne fori argentei aleator?*
Is the Midland Bank a joint-stock company?	*Argentaria Mediterranea estne societas collocatae pecuniae?*
Just like the other big banks.	*pariter atque ceterae mensae magnae.*
A limited partnership.	*societas commendatoria.*
A limited company.	*societas sponsionis limitatae.*

How large is the original stock? *quantus est eius fundus pecuniarius?*

£30,000,000; the bank guarantees this amount. *trecenties centena milia librarum Anglicarum; qua re spondet mensa.*

Security. *sponsio.*

A safe

The Bank of England issues notes and coins. *Anglica Mensa Publica nummarias chartulas et nummos edit.*

It supervises the circulation of money. *pecuniis commercandis commutandisque invigilat.*

It accepts good bills of exchange from the banks. *bonas pecuniae syngraphas a mensis accipit.*

It fixes the rate for discounting bills. *magnitudinem deductionis syngraphae constituit.*

A cheque.	*perscriptio.*
A dividend.	*lucri portio.*
A savings book.	*libellus pecuniae.*
A savings bank.	*aerariŭm pecūlii (cum ūsūrā) conficiendi.*
A safe (strong-box).	*armarium nummarium (vel loricatum).*
Exchange-office (Bureau de Change).	*(publica) pecuniae (vel nummorum) permutatio.*
Money-changer.	*nummularius.*
Cashier.	*arcarius (vel dispensator)*
Premium (Agio).	*collȳbus, i m.*
Italian Lire.	*nummi Italici (vel libellae Italicae).*
Pounds sterling.	*librae Anglicae.*
The dollar.	*nummus Americanus.*
Revaluation.	*revaloratio.*
Devaluation.	*devaloratio.*

At the Railway Station — in ferratae viae statione

Here we are at the station.	*nos hic in statione ferriviaria!*
We're in good time.	*in tempore adsumus.*
The railway staff are very friendly and helpful to travellers.	*ferratae viae addicti magna cum comitate adiuvant viatores.*
Please call a porter.	*advoca, quaeso, gerulum!*
Please tell me where the ticket office is.	*dic mihi, quaeso, ubi tesserae viatoriae veneant!*
The ticket office is to the right of the entrance.	*tesserarum diribitorium dextra a parte introitus est.*
A first-class return ticket for the express, please.	*itus et reditus tessĕram ordinis primi peto hamaxostĭcho citissimo.*
Where to?	*quonam?*

To Birmingham.	*Birminghamiam.*
Local train.	*hamaxostichus communis.*
Fast train.	*hamaxostichus citus.*
Express train (Inter-city).	*hamaxostichus rapidus.*
We must go through the subway.	*per cuniculum nobis est eundum.*
There's the Station-master.	*ecce stationis praepositus!*
Hasn't the Birmingham train arrived yet?	*nonne hamaxostichus Birminghamiensis advenit?*
It'll be here approximately fifteen minutes later than usual.	*plus minus quindecim minūtis solito serius intrabit.*
In that case I've plenty of time.	*quae cum ita sint, multum mihi erit temporis.*
Meanwhile I'll smoke a cigarette.	*interea nicotianam succendam fistulam.*
Oh dear! I've left my lighter at home.	*eheu, igniarium domi est relictum.*
You can buy some matches either at the station restaurant or from that vendor over there.	*fac emas ramenta sulphurata vel in stationis caupona vel de isto institore!*
Do you see the steam-engine with a tender over there?	*videsne istam machinam vectoriam (vapore actam) cum plaustro carbonario?*
Such machines are used for shunting.	*tales machinae ad agmen curruum componendum usurpantur.*
Passenger carriage.	*viatorum currus.*
Luggage van.	*currus sarcinarius (vel onerarius).*
Restaurant car.	*currus cenatorius (vel escarius).*
Sleeping car.	*currus dormitorius.*

Post and Telegraph	**de cursu publico et telegrăpho**
Haven't you had a letter?	*nihilne litterarum accepisti?* / *nullaene tibi sunt redditae litterae?*
I haven't received a letter.	*litterarum nihil accepi.*
Money would be more welcome than a letter where I'm concerned.	*equidem pecunias accipere malim quam litteras.*
I'm not worried about the letter provided that the money comes.	*nihil moror litteras, argentum modo veniat.*
Ask the postman if he has any letters for me.	*interrŏga tabellarium, quid mihi habeat litterarum.*
Here's a letter for you.	*cape epistulam!*
It has been stamped with two 3p stamps.	*duobus pittaciis cursualibus* (*vel vehiculariis*) *ternariis munita est.*
Open the letter.	*solve* (*vel aperi*) *epistulam!*
What does the letter say?	*quid hae loquuntur litterae?*
I can't decipher it.	*non possum has nŏtas dinōscere.*
I can; he and I have been writing to each other for a long time.	*ego possum; diu enim cum eo per litteras collocutus sum.*
I've just had a telegram announcing my sister's engagement.	*modo mihi nuntiatum est telegraphice sororem meam esse desponsam.*
I'll write a letter (send a telegram) at once to congratulate her.	*statim per litteras* (*per telegraphum*) *ei gratulabor.*
Express post.	*citissimus nuntius.*
Shall I telegraph the news to our friend?	*visne amico nostro telephonice nuntiem?*
The Telegraph Office is in the Post Office building.	*sedes nostra telegraphica* (*vel telegraphīum*) *est in publico epistularum diribitorio.*

Take this registered letter to the Post Office, and buy a television licence at the same time.	*ad epistularum diribitorium perfer hanc epistulam commendatam et simul solve stipem televisoriam.*
Post the letter in a letter-box.	*in publici cursus capsulam epistulam demitte!*
Postal charges have gone up.	*publici cursus pretia aucta sunt.*
Wireless telegraph.	*radiotelegráphĭa.*
Airmail.	*epistula aërіā viā missa.*
A teleprinter.	*machina telegraphica.*
A stamp.	*pittacium cursale (vel p. vehicularium)*
To stamp a letter.	*epistulam pittacio vehiculario munire.*
A postcard.	*charta (vel chartula) cursualis.*
A picture postcard.	*publici cursus chartula (vel scidula) lucis ope picta.*
An envelope.	*involucrum.*
A postal order.	*nummarium publici cursus mandatum (vel nummaria c. p. chartula vel scidula).*
A postmark.	*sigillum (vel signum) cursuale (vel vehicularium).*
A stamp-collector.	*philatelista.*
An unused stamp.	*pittacium integrum.*
A used stamp.	*pittacium signatum.*
A special issue.	*pittacium peculiare.*
Correspondence.	*commercium epistŭlare.*
A stamp-album.	*libellus albarum paginarum laqueatarum.*

Travelling — in itinĕre

He is away from home.	*peregrinatur.*
He is abroad.	*perĕgre est.*

He has left a young wife and a number of children at home. — *domi habet uxorem intĕgra adhuc aetate et aliquot liberos.*

What are they doing meanwhile? — *quid illi agunt interim?*

They've gone on holiday. — *rusticatum abierunt.*

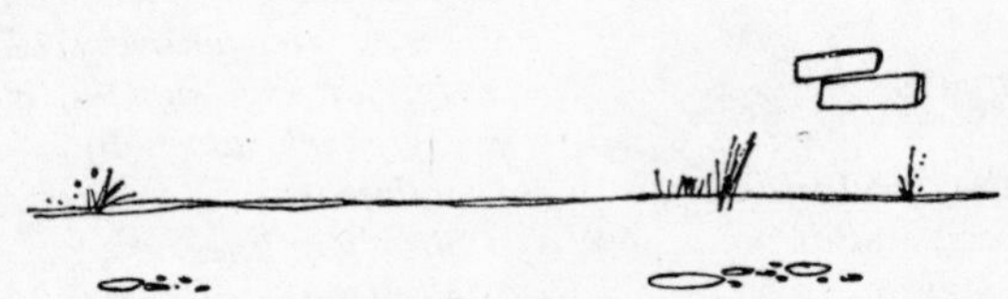

Is there anything worth seeing there?

What are you doing here? — *quid tu hic agis?*

I'm going to have a look at Switzerland. — *Helvetiam lustrabo.*

We need a rest. — *relaxationem animi quaerimus.*

We must leave at once. — *e vestigio profiscendum est nobis!*

Where have you come from? — *unde venītis?*

From Brindisi. From Corfu. — *Brundisio venīmus. – Corcȳra.*

From so far away? — *e tam longinquo?*

That's right.	*sic est.*
Is there anything worth seeing there?	*estne illic, quod tu putes spectatu dignum?*
What a thing to ask! Corfu is a paradise.	*heus quid tu? Corcyra est quasi Elysium!*
Nowhere on earth are the people more friendly.	*nusquam terrarum homines hospitaliores.*
But what are the hotels like?	*sed deversoria qualia?*
The 'Ωραία (= beautiful) Βενετία is first-class.	*deversorium Corcyraeum, quod dicitur 'Bella Venetia', est eximium.*
Were you sea-sick on the crossing from Brindisi?	*nausĕastīne, cum Brundisio transvehereris?*
Yes, I was. The Adriatic can certainly be rough.	*non sine nausea navigavi. nempe turbidum Hadriaticum (mare).*
But it's pleasant to recall troubles that are over.	*sed iucundum est meminisse laborum actorum.*
Another advantage of travel is that it makes one appreciate home more afterwards.	*hoc quoque commoditatis habet peregrinatio, quod dulcior est postea domus.*
How long have you been away from home?	*quantum temporis afuisti domo?*
Nearly six months.	*iam sex ferme menses.*
Where have you been all this time?	*ubi tam diu peregrinatus es?*
I've been studying in Berlin.	*Berolini litteris cognoscendis studui.*
Give my regards to all my friends.	*meo nomine (vel meis verbis) salutes omnes amicos meos!*
By all means.	*id quidem fiet.*
Have a good journey.	*bene ambula!*
Good-bye.	*bene vale!*

Summer Holidays	**de itinĕre aestivo**
Where are you off to this summer?	*quo hac aestate profecturus es?*
I haven't made up my mind whether to go to the Harz Forest or the sea.	*nondum scio, utrum in Silvam Hercyniam an ad litus maris proficiscar.*
Do you know the North Sea and the Baltic?	*novistine mare Germanicum et mare Balticum?*
The North Sea is more stormy, the Baltic calmer; the former is tidal, the latter is practically tideless.	*illud turbulentius, hoc placidius est; illud aestuum recessum et accessum habet, hoc his commutationibus paene caret.*
Sea bathing is very healthy.	*lavationes in mari factae saluberrimae sunt.*
The islands are reached by steamer.	*insulas navibus vapore motis (vel vaporariis) petimus.*
The Harz Forest around the Brocken is marvellous too.	*Silva Hercynia quoque circa montem Bructerum sita praeclara est.*
There one can hide oneself in the thick forest.	*ibi in silvam densam nos abstrudere possumus.*
And I don't emerge again before evening.	*tum inde non exeo ante vesperum.*
Nothing does me more good than solitude.	*nihil mihi salubrius est solitudine.*
It gives me real physical and mental relaxation.	*ea vera corporis et animi relaxatio est.*
All around there are shady woods, green meadows and bubbling springs.	*nusquam ibi desunt nemoris umbra, prata vĭrĭdia, fontium scătĕbrae.*
I tend to get up very early.	*prima luce resurgere soleo.*
Then I go for a walk in the forest.	*tum in silva ambulo.*
The attraction of the area lies in the beauty of its hills and valleys.	*regio pulchritudine collium et vallium amoenissima est.*

But nature alone does not satisfy me; the mind needs books and newspapers too.	*nec tamen natura sola mihi satisfacit; libris quoque et ephemeridibus animus eget.*
At night I sleep with the window open, so as always to have fresh air.	*noctu fenestris apertis dormio, ut respirans semper āere recenti utar.*
I hope to return home soon refreshed in body and mind.	*me mox corpore animoque corroboratum domum reversurum esse spero.*
I'm sure that the daily round will give me more pleasure than before.	*tum officia diurna mihi maiori gaudio quam antea fore certo scio.*

In the Hotel Bedroom	**in cubiculo dormitorio**
The bedroom.	*cubĭculum dormitorium.*
I stayed up late yesterday.	*vigilavi heri diu.*
I'm tired from the journey and I'm going to bed.	*ex itinĕre lassus petam lectum.*
Wait till the others go to bed too.	*exspecta, dum ceteri eant cubĭtum.*
How clean it is here!	*quanta hic mundities est!*
The sheets are clean and there are fresh pillow-cases.	*linteum lautum est et pulvīni quoque recentibus involūcris sunt inducti.*
What a smart new hotel with running hot and cold water in all rooms!	*deversorium novum elegansque cum aqua frigida et calida in omnibus conclavibus fluente!*
Let's go to bed.	*cubĭtum eamus!*
Where's my night-shirt? (where are my pyjamas?)	*ŭbi est tunica (vel vestis) mea nocturna?*
The hall porter will call us.	*ianĭtor nos excitabit.*
Here's the light switch.	*hic lumen electricum exstinguitur.*
The bed is badly made.	*lectus male stratus est.*

I can't get to sleep.	*somnum capere non possum.*
He's fast asleep already.	*iam artē dormit.*
Have you locked the door?	*obserastīne ostium?*
Who's knocking at the door?	*quis pulsat ostium?*
Shut the door (window).	*ostium (fenestram) claude!*
Open the door.	*ostium apĕri!*
I'll only open the window a tiny bit.	*aperiam rimam fenestrae.*

On the Main Road — media in via primaria

How many miles is it to the nearest town?	*quot milia sunt usque ad proximum oppidum?*
Approximately twenty.	*ad viginti.*
Is there a garage there?	*estne ibi autovehiculorum statio?*
Right by the first group of houses.	*prima inter ipsa aedificia.*
Is there a good workshop in the neighbourhood?	*estne in propinquo (vel proximo) officina vehiculis sarciendis?*
Not as far as I know.	*quantum scio, non est.*
My tank's almost empty.	*benzīni receptaculum meum vacuum fere est.*
Be so kind, and let me have a little petrol.	*da mihi hanc veniam, ut tradas mihi paulum benzīni!*
How much do you need?	*quanto eges?*
A gallon if possible.	*des congium, si poteris.*
With pleasure.	*libentissimo animo.*
One of my tyres is damaged.	*unus ex canthis pneumaticis (vel cummeis) est laesus.*
Would you lend me your jack for a few minutes?	*commodabisne mihi trochleam paucas minutas?*
And a screwdriver?	*etiamne capulum cochleis (con)torquendis?*

The pneumatic pump.	*antlia pneumatica.*
Very many thanks.	*gratias ago quam maximas.*
The road is closed at two points.	*duobus locis via est praeclusa.*
You'll have to make two detours along side-roads.	*bis obliquis itineribus cogēris circumire.*

The road is closed at two points

Once again many thanks.	*iterum gratiam maximam.*
All the best.	*optima quaeque tibi precor.*

In the Workshop — **in officina vehicŭlis sarciendis**

Are you working long today?	*laborabitisne diu hodie?*
We close at six.	*sexta hora officinam claudemus.*

We'll give your car a thorough examination tomorrow morning.	*cras mane accuratissime perquiremus vehiculum tuum.*
In particular check the brakes, the steering and the cooling system.	*imprimis velim sufflamina (vel frenos), axem moderaminis, refrigeratorium inspiciatis.*
There's a big garage opposite the town hall.	*curiae adversum magna autoraedarum statio est.*
They deal with all types of vehicles.	*ibi vehicula omne genus collocantur.*
A motor-car.	*automataria raeda (vel autoraeda, autovehiculum)*
A limousine.	*automataria carruca.*
The hodometer.	*itineris metiendi index.*
The speedometer.	*velocitatis index.*
A lorry.	*autocurrus, automatarius currus (vel plaustrum automatarium).*
A bus.	*automatarium petorritum.*
A coach.	*automătum Pullmannianum.*
A motorist.	*autoraedarius.*
An armoured-car.	*automatarius covinnus (vel currus armatus, ignivŏmus).*

How are things? (Health and Business) — quid agis? (de valetudine, de arte)

How are you?	*quid agis?*
How are you feeling?	*valesne?*
I'm not asking how you're feeling; for it's clear from your face that you're very well.	*non interrogo, ut valeas, nam facies ipsa loquitur te belle valere.*
How is business?	*satín' salvae?* (sc. *sunt res tuae?*)
Not too bad.	*rebus meis contentus sum.*

How are things at work? Are you satisfied?	*quo pacto se res habent tuae? satin' ex sententia?*
Are things going well for you?	*satin' salva omnia?*
Are things going as well as you could wish?	*satisne prospera omnia?*
Things couldn't be worse.	*res in peiore statu esse non potest.*
I feel wretched.	*aegre est mihi.*
You haven't achieved your aim?	*non consecutus es, quod volebas?*
Is there no hope left?	*nihil reliquum est spei?*
There's plenty of hope, but nothing to go on.	*spei permultum, sed rei nihil.*
So we must live on our hopes.	*ergo spe alendus est animus.*
But hope doesn't fill the stomach.	*neque tamen hac saginatur venter!* (*saginare* to fatten).
Where are you going from here?	*quo nunc hinc abis?*
Straight home.	*rectā domum.*
I hope that you find everything in order there.	*precor, ut illic offendas omnia laeta.*
God grant I do.	*utinam ita velit Deus!*

Ill Health	**de valetudine mala**
Are you quite well?	*rectēne vales?*
Would that I were!	*vellem quidem!*
Not quite as I could wish.	*non admodum ex sententia.*
So, so.	*sic satis.*
Not as well as I might be.	*non optime sane.*
Worse than ever.	*sic, ut antehac peius numquam.*
I'm in my usual state of health.	*valeo, ut solitus sum.*
How do you feel?	*quomodo vales?*
Less well than I could wish.	*secus quam vellem.*
How's your health?	*qua valetudine es?*

Not very good.	*parum prosperā.*
Tolerable.	*tolerabili.*
Fairish.	*vix mediŏcri.*
Bad.	*malā* (*vel adversā*).
Not good.	*haud sane commodā.* (*vel incommodā.*)

They all say different things but there's a general agreement that I'm in a bad way

Uncertain.	*dubiā.*
Oh dear!	*quod avertat Deus!* *bona verba!*
You must keep your spirits up.	*bono sis animo oportet!*
He has a cough.	*tussit.*
In heaven's name, what's the matter with you?	*amabo, quid tibi est?*
I'll fetch a doctor.	*arcessam medicum.*
How are your spirits?	*quid tibi animi est?*

My foot's hurting.	*pes mihi dolet.*
The pain is easing.	*dolores remittunt.*
What sort of a pain is it?	*quod mali genus est?*
What's wrong with you?	*quid habes morbi?* *qui te tenet morbus?* *quo morbo tenēris?*
I don't know.	*nescio.*
Haven't you seen a doctor?	*nullumne consuluisti medicum?*
Oh yes! I've seen lots.	*equidem multos.*
And what do they say?	*quid respondent?*
They all say different things, but there's a general agreement that I'm in a bad way.	*alius aliud dicit; neque quisquam me miserum esse negat.*
How long have you been feeling unwell?	*ex quo tempore hoc morbo affectus es?*
About three weeks.	*dies plus minus viginti.*
Almost a month.	*ferme mensis est.*
Over two months.	*iam tertius est mensis.*
Where do you think that you picked up the disease?	*unde suspicaris hoc esse collectum mali?*
He sneezed.	*sternuit.*
He keeps on sneezing.	*sternūtat.*
Bless you!	*salve!*
Your health!	*sit faustum ac felix!*
God save us!	*bene vertat Deus!*
I've a streaming cold.	*nares gravedine vexantur.*
I think it started with a cold.	*e perfrīctione natum* (*esse*) *arbitror.*
It couldn't have come from drinking too much, could it?	*vide, ne ex potatione largiore!*
Take a laxative.	*sume, quod alvum deiciat!*
What I need is something to stop me; I've got diarrhoea.	*immo sistat, nam plus, quam satis est, profluit.*
He is seriously ill.	*gravi morbo aeger est* (*Liv. 42, 28, 11*) *vel gr. m. implicatus est.*
He is partially crippled.	*parte membrorum captus est.*

He is completely crippled.	*omnibus membris captus est.*
I'm perfectly well.	*bene est (mihi).*
I'm feeling better.	*melius mihi est.*
I'm feeling a little better.	*meliuscule mihi est.*
I've recovered.	*melius mihi est factum.*
I've always been in good health.	*semper prospera (vel bona) valetudine sum usus.* *usque adhuc integra valetudine fui.*
I'm pleased to hear it.	*laetus (vel haud invitus) istuc audio.*
God grant that it's always so.	*faxit deus, ut istuc sit perpetuum.*
I'm absolutely delighted to hear you say that.	*est istuc mihi auditu perquam iucundum.*
I thank God for it.	*gratiam habeo Deo.*

In a Doctor's Surgery	**in medici conclavi consultationum**
Whose turn is it?	*quisnam sequitur?*
Come in.	*intra!*
As a matter of fact you arrived after me, but as you look ill you can go in before me. I don't mind waiting.	*quamquam post me advenisti, tamen, quia languidus esse videris, quaeso ante me intra! Opperiri me non piget.*
Very kind of you. Thank you.	*bene! Gratias!*
What's the trouble?	*quo morbo laboras?*
I don't know. There's a pain in my stomach and bowels.	*nescio; stomăcho visceribusque doleo.*
You look pale; you could be anaemic.	*pallidus es; sanguine recte composito egere videris.*
What illnesses have you had?	*quibus es morbis perfunctus?*
I had almost all the usual children's illnesses: whooping	*omnes fere morbos transii pueriles: tussi clangosa, rha-*

cough, rickets, measles, scarlet fever and several bouts of tonsillitis.	*chitĭde, morbillis, scarlatīna, saepius tonsillis inflammatis laboravi.*
Have you ever had an operation?	*iamne aliquando scalpello es sectus?*

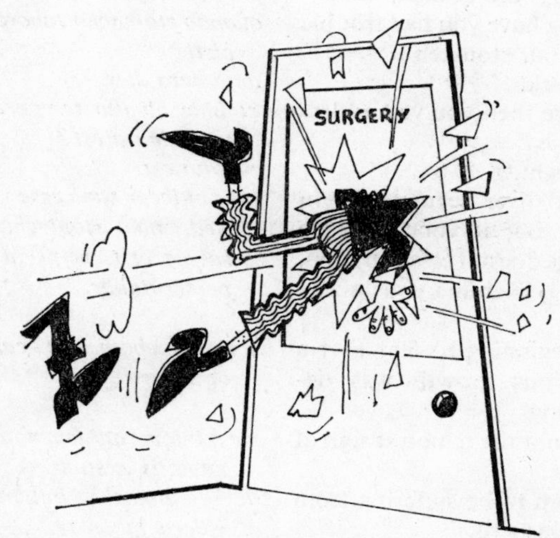

As a matter of fact you arrived after me, but as you look ill you can go in before me . . .

After recovering from appendicitis, I had my appendix removed.	*appendicitĭde bene superata fŭndulus exsectus est.*
I'll give you a rather more thorough examination.	*rem paulo accuratius explorabo.*
Get undressed.	*vestem exue!*
I'm going to listen to your chest.	*pectus tuum sono digiti vel malleŏli explorabo.*
And I want to listen to your heart-beat.	*cordis quoque sonos scrutabor.*

Please sit down.	*assidas velim!*
Take deep breaths.	*profundē aërem respira et redde!*
Your heart-beat is normal.	*soni cordis tui naturae respondent.*
Your lungs are in order too.	*pulmones quoque sani sunt.*
How long have you had trouble with your stomach?	*quando stomacho laborare coepisti?*
For a week.	*ante octo dies.*
And since then you've had less appetite?	*et inde ab illo tempore fames tua minuta est?*
That's right.	*minuta est.*
Gall and liver seem to be in order. But if your stomach trouble doesn't clear up soon, I'll also examine your abdomen.	*bilis et iecur sana esse videntur. Sed, nisi stomachus brevi salvus erit, ventrem quoque perscrutabor.*
I was beginning to fear that a cancerous growth was developing.	*iam timebam, ne carcinōma oreretur.*
There's not the remotest sign of cancer.	*ne minimae quidem notae carcinomătis exstant.*
You seem to be suffering from mild gastritis.	*levi stomachi inflammatione videris laborare.*
It may prove necessary to make an X-ray examination.	*fortasse per radios Roentgenios ventrem opus erit introspicere.*
For the time being we'll try and get your digestion in order, and I'll prescribe you a medicine for that.	*interim stomachum ad cibos concoquendos stimulabo, quam ad rem efficiendam medicamentum tibi praescribam.*
Here's the prescription. Take twenty drops in water three times a day before meals. The medicine is available from chemists.	*en scida officinalis! Ter cottidie ante cenam viginti guttae aqua dilūtae sumendae sunt. Hoc remedium in pharmacopoliis suppetit.*

Thank you. When do you want to see me again?	*gratias ago; quando mihi reveniendum est?*
In a few days if things don't get any worse, which I'm not expecting. Rather I'm expecting your appetite to improve.	*intra paucos dies, nisi res in peius mutabitur, quod futurum esse non puto. Quin potius cupiditas tua edendi augebitur.*
Good-bye.	*vale!*

At the Sick-bed — ad aegroti lectum

How did you sleep?	*quomodo dormivisti?*
Badly, but it was kind of you to ask.	*gratias, male.*
May I take your pulse?	*pulsum arteriarum quaeso porrige!*
It's still too fast, but it's firm and regular.	*etiam nunc valde acceleratus est, sed firmus et aequalis.*
Did you wrap yourself in a cold compress according to my instructions, and have a good sweat?	*involvistine fomento frigido corpus praecepta mea secutus involutusque valde sudavisti?*
I did.	*feci et sudavi!*
Did you take your temperature yesterday evening?	*num heri vespertino tempore corporis calorem mensus es?*
And again this morning?	*et hodie quoque matutino tempore?*
I did.	*mensus sum!*
There we are! Your temperature's a whole degree lower today, which is perfectly natural.	*ecce! Calorem toto gradu minorem hodie cognoscimus, quod naturae conveniens est.*
Your temperature will probably go up this evening, but you're getting better.	*febris hodie tempore vespertino fortasse augebitur; morbus autem diminuetur.*

I'll call again tomorrow.	*cras iterum revertar.*
You'll probably be able to get up within the next few days.	*proximis diebus te resurgere posse existimo.*

An Operation — de sectione chirurgica

I don't think that I'll be able to save the whole of your finger; you've come to me too late.	*totum digitum tuum a me conservari posse non puto; sero ad me venisti.*
Oh dear! Will it have to be amputated?	*vae mihi! Num amputandus est?*
It's lucky that it's the left hand.	*bene accidit, quod est manus sinistra.*
That's some consolation.	*ergo solacio utaris!*
But the finger-tip is septic.	*sed extremus digitus sanie iam deletus est.*
Look, there's pus coming out.	*ecce, pus emānat.*
Surely you don't want blood-poisoning?	*num sanguinem infĭci vis?*
So be brave!	*ergo bono sis animo!*
I'm sure you're in great pain, but I'll rid you of it. The operation itself will be almost painless.	*te magnis doloribus cruciari puto, quibus te liberabo; ipsa autem resectio paene sine doloribus fiet.*
I'll just make a call to a colleague who'll be here very shortly.	*confestim telephonicē collegae rem nuntiabo, qui brevissimo tempore aderit.*
And then we can start.	*quo facto incipiemus.*
You're a strong, healthy fellow.	*homo validus et robustus es.*
There are worse cases.	*res peiores eveniunt.*
Even with one finger-tip missing you'll be able to hold an object in your left hand.	*manu sinistra, etiamsi cuiusdam digiti extremi particula deest, rem aliquam retinere poteris.*
In ten days the finger will have	*decem diebus peractis digitus*

healed; for we shall only remove the tip.	*sanus erit; nam nihil nisi membrum extremum amputabimus.*
Here's my colleague.	*ecce collega!*
Good day to you.	*salve, collega!*
There's no need to put you to sleep; we'll only use a local anaesthetic.	*digitum sensu carentem neque totum corpus torpentem reddere volumus.*
But stay and give me a hand all the same please.	*attamen, collega, ut mihi assistas, hīc quaeso remane!*
With pleasure.	*libenter remaneo.*
There! All over!	*en! Res finita est.*
And you must not use your left hand for ten days. Understood?	*et tibi per decem dies manu sinistra non est utendum. Intellexistine?*
Meanwhile come to my surgery every other day, so that I can look at the finger and see that it's healing properly.	*interea alternis diebus hora consultationum ad me veni, ut digitum inspicere sanationemque observare possim!*

Billiards	**de arte pilis eburneis ludendi**
Let's play billiards.	*sphaeris eburnĕis ludamus.*
Shall we toss to decide who starts?	*visne sortiamur, uter prior incipiat?*
It's only fair that a great billiard-player like yourself should give me a start of a few points.	*aequum est te tantum in hoc certamine artificem mihi largiri nonnihil.*
But it's not particularly honourable to owe one's success to the generosity of one's opponent.	*sed parum honesta est victoria precaria.*
Play!	*feri!*
I'll drive you out from there!	*istinc te excutiam!*
You can only do that by mak-	*non potes alia via, nisi sic mit-*

ing your ball rebound into mine from the cushion.

tas sphaeram tuam in parietem, ut resiliat in meam.

I'll try it.

id experiar.

What do you say to that, my dear fellow? That shifted you, didn't it?

quid ais, bone vir? nonne depulsus es?

But it's not particularly honourable to owe one's success to the generosity of one's opponent . . .

You know perfectly well how to do it!

quo pacto id fieri soleat, calles!

But one can try that hundreds of times, and it will hardly work once.

sed istuc sescenties temptanti vix semel succedet.

Bowling

de conorum ludo (vel de coniludio)

Let's go bowling.

cōnorum ludum faciamus.

I've no objection.

age nihil moror (non moror).

There's no better exercise for all parts of the body than bowling.

nulla re melius exercentur omnes corporis partes quam glŏbis ligněis mittendis.

But it's a more suitable pastime for winter than for summer, for in winter one sweats less.	*sed aptior hic lusus hiemi quam aestati, nam hieme minus sudatur.*
How much shall we play for?	*quanti certabimus?*
For a rap on the knuckles.	*tālĭtrō.*
There must be something at stake; otherwise the game becomes boring.	*aliquo periculo certandum est; aliōqui friget ludus.*
You're right.	*sic res se habet, ut dicis.*
The losing side will pay the winners one pound.	*utra pars vicerit, ei victa solvet libram.*
But only on condition that all the winnings are used to pay for a party to which all the players are invited.	*sed hac condicione, ut, quidquid ex victoriis collectum erit, insumatur in convivium, ad quod pariter vocentur omnes.*
A good condition. I accept it.	*placet lex et rata esto.*
All we have to do now is draw lots for sides.	*superest igitur, ut sortiamur partes.*
We're all so nearly equal that it doesn't matter who plays on which side.	*sumus pares ferme omnes, ut non magni rēfĕrat, cui quis coniungatur.*
But you've had far more practice than I have.	*tu tamen me multo peritior es.*
Be that as it may, but you have more luck.	*ut sim, at tu felicior.*
Does luck matter even here?	*fortuna etiam hic valet?*
It's supreme everywhere.	*illa nusquam non regnat.*
Let's proceed with the lot.	*age, fiat sortitio.*
Hurrah! We have been lucky.	*euge, bene cecĭdit!*
We've got the side I wanted.	*coniuncti sunt, quos volebam.*
We're not dissatisfied with our team either.	*nos quoque nostrae sodalitatis non paenitet.*
You won't have reason to complain about me.	*laudabis me.*
A throw that grazes the board doesn't count.	*qui ad crepidinem miserit, frustra misit.*

Three! (sc. knocked over).	*ternio (sc. effecta est)!*
Four! Five! Six!	*quaternio! quinio! senio!*
All nine!	*io novenio!*
He's a lucky fellow!	*hominem felicem!*
It went better than I expected.	*res successit opinione melius.*
Luck was on your side.	*fortuna tibi favit.*
Everything turns out as you wish.	*ex sententia tibi cadunt omnia.*
It all went perfectly for me.	*res omnis cecĭdit ex sententia.*
Let's have a return match.	*par pari referamus.*
I'll make an effort.	*dabitur opera.*
You'll do your best to help me.	*tu me, quoad poteris, adiutabis!*
We have won 30.	*vicimus triginta.*
Pence?	*nummos?*
No.	*non.*
What then?	*quid igitur?*
Points.	*numeros.*
This game's in the bag.	*noster est hic ludus.*
You're crowing too soon.	*praepropĕre tu quidem triumphas.*
This is the crucial point.	*nunc res agitur!*
What a brilliant throw!	*egregius profecto iactus!*
He's not much good when all the pins are standing.	*in pleno conorum numero nihil efficit.*
He aims at single pins and knocks them down.	*singulos petit et subvertit.*
He has left a lot of isolated pins.	*sparsos relīquit conos!*
Your throw.	*mitte!*
Aim at the king-pin! At the one in front! At the pin in the right-hand (left-hand) corner!	*pete regem! primum! dextimum! sinistimum!* (actually the one furthest to the right or left as the case may be).
Now things are getting serious!	*nunc naviter res agitur!*
Hurrah! Success!	*euge, successit!*

Didn't I tell you?	*dixin'?* (*Plaut.*; otherwise:) *nōnne dixi?*
What a wizard you are!	*o magum egregium!*
We're even!	*aequali fortuna sumus.*
We've won!	*vicimus! vel: penes nos est huius certaminis victoria!*
Chalk up our winnings so that they're not forgotten.	*scribe lucrum nostrum creta, ne nobis excĭdat.*
It would be better to stop playing so as not to overdo it.	*praestat a ludo desistere; ne quid nimis.*
Let's reckon up the winnings.	*computemus lucrum.*
Our accounts agree.	*ratio constat.*
We've won three pounds, and you've won two.	*nos vicimus tres libras, vos duas.*
That leaves one for a little drink.	*restat igitur una ad compotatiunculam.*
But who's going to pay the bowling fee?	*sed interim quis solvet pretium conōrum?*
Everyone must pay his own share.	*omnes ex aequo, pro sua quisque portione.*
Yes, the winnings are too small to take anything from them.	*lucrum enim exilius est, quam ut demi quicquam possit.*

Another Game — de alio ludo (vel lusu)

Chess.	*ludus scaccorum.*
To play chess.	*scaccis ludere.*

NB: These expressions are non-Classical. The ancient *ludus latrunculorum* was not chess.

Check!	*cave regi!*
Bishop. Knight. Castle.	*cursor. caballus. turris.*
Pawns.	*latrunculi* (*vel milites vel latrones*).
To checkmate.	*ad incitas redigere.*

Playing Cards	**de chartarum ludicro**
Wasting one's time and money on games of chance is a sordid form of amusement.	*illiberalis est voluptas aleā tempus et rem perdere.*
Let's play cards then.	*pagĭnis igitur ludamus!* (*chartŭlis lūsoriis*)

NB: These terms come from mediaeval monastic sources; in Classical times cards were not played.

He is a very good card player.	*peritissimus est lusūs paginarum.*
In this respect he is more accomplished than I could wish.	*hac in parte plus praestat quam velim.*
Shall we try our luck?	*visne fortunam experiamur?*
How much do you play for?	*quanti luditis?*
We only play to pass the time.	*consumendi otii causa ludimus.*
For relaxation; for pleasure.	*animi causa.*
I'm sorry for you.	*vestri me miseret!*
I have grim forebodings.	*animus praesāgit mihi aliquid mali!*
Let's get on with it.	*quid cessas?*
You were right there.	*istuc recte.*
Well done.	*bene factum!*
Superlative.	*nihil supra!*
That's right. Splendid.	*laudo! optime!*
That was silly of me.	*factum a me stulte est!*
I've been too stupid.	*nimis insipiens fui!*
I've lost.	*acta haec res est!*
Oh dear! Oh dear!	*perii!*
We've lost the game.	*actum est!*
What do you intend to do now?	*quid nunc facere cogitas?*
I've made a mistake, I admit.	*peccavi, fateor.*
That's enough. I don't want any more.	*pax! nihil amplius.*
So I got excited about nothing.	*ah, frustra sum igitur gavisus!*
I'm finished.	*occĭdi!*

Oh, unfortunate wretch that I am!	*vae misero mihi!*
You're not going to get away with that.	*haud inultum hoc feres!*
Now I simply don't know what to do.	*nunc, quo me vertam, nescio!*
Come on! Hurry up!	*age!* (*vel rumpe moram!*).
What can you be thinking of to make a fool of us in this way?	*quid tibi venit in mentem, ut nos ad istum modum ludos facias?*
Just at the right moment!	*commodum profecto!*
I smell a rat.	*subŏlet* (*mihi*)*!*
That's the end. There's nothing more we can do.	*actum est; ilĭcet!*
I fell into the trap.	*captus sum!*
All right then! I'll get my own back.	*age, par pari referam!*
You made a serious mistake.	*peccatum a* (= *abs*) *te maxime est.*
What's the point of all this?	*quorsum spectant haec omnia?*
What's this leading to, may I ask?	*ad quid hoc tandem condūcit?*
What's the good of that?	*quorsum hoc valet?*
What use is that?	*ad quid hoc proficit?*
What's the advantage in that?	*quid hoc emolumenti habet?*
Who profits from that?	*cui bono?*
It turned out otherwise than I had expected.	*res aliter cecĭdit ac putaveram.*
Now it all depends on you.	*nunc in te omnia sunt!*
Now is a favourable moment.	*nunc occasio datur!*
You've missed your chance.	*occasionem praetermisisti!*
Now take your opportunity.	*nunc occasionem arrĭpe!*
I'm not sure what I should do.	*metuo, quid faciam.*
You're lucky.	*fortuna tibi est* (*Liv.* 36, 19, 1). *fortuna secunda utĕris!* *prospero fortunae flatu utĕris!* (*Cic. Off.* 2, 6, 19).

You're unlucky.	*a Fortuna derelictus es!*
Good luck.	*bene id tibi vertat!*
This is war.	*haec est alea Martis!*
Now it's death or glory.	*nunc necesse est stare aut occasurum aut occisurum.*

A miracle! We've won

What will become of us?	*quid (de) nobis fiet?*
It's all up with us.	*actum est de nobis!*
I'm very hopeful of victory.	*magna me spes tenet nos victuros esse.*
We can draw fresh hope.	*spem redintegrare licet.*
A miracle! We've won!	*divinitus accidit! vicimus!*
I've had enough of this session.	*iam taedet me sessionis!*

Sport	**de ludicris corporis exercitationibus**
(a) BALL-GAMES	(*a*) *DE LUSIONIBUS PILARIBUS*
Do you play any games?	*exercesne corpus tuum?*
I'm an active member of a sports club.	*sodalis actuosus societatis sum athleticae.*
Did your enthusiasm for games start when you were a boy?	*erasne iam puer ludicrorum studiosissimus?*
I greatly enjoyed playing ball-games.	*summo studio follis ludis (folliludiis) intereram.*
'Ball-games are suitable for boys and old men,' as the Roman poet Martial said (Ep. 14, 47).	*'folle decet pueros ludere, folle senes,' iam dixit Martialis poeta Romanus.*
I was always particularly keen on football.	*follis pede pulsandi eram cupidissimus.*
What position did you play in your team?	*quonam eras loco vestro in agmine?*
I was generally outside left, while my brother played in goal.	*plerumque comes in laeva manu eram, cum frater esset ianitor retis.*
Finally I was centre forward and captain of the side as well.	*postremo medius incursor fui atque etiam agminis dux.*
The trainer did all he could to improve our play.	*instructor noster impigre nos expolīvit.*
Recently I watched a match between Liverpool and Manchester United.	*in campo lusorio nuper spectavi certamen inter Liverpolienses et Mancunienses Unitos.*
With what skill George Best intercepted the ball, controlled it through the attempted tackles of the opposition and drove it into the net from far out.	*qua sollertia follem intercepit Georgius ille Optimus, per adversantium occursus rexit, victor in alterum rete propulit.*

Our goalkeeper was severely kicked by an opponent, but the referee ignored the offence.
ianitor retis noster calcem ab adversario accepit gravem, sed iniuriam non persecutus est arbiter.

The fellow needs new spectacles.
opus est isti novis perspicillis.

Our goalkeeper was severely kicked by an opponent, but the referee ignored the offence

The match was drawn.
aequo Marte certatum est.

I preferred to play hand-ball.
egomet pila manuāli ludere malebam.

I have to keep running, jumping, throwing.
cogor assidue currere, salire, iacĕre.

In school we often used a punch-ball.
in schola saepe follem feriebamus pugnis.

A punch-ball.
follis pugillatorius (Plaut. Rud. 3, 4, 16).

Recently I've joined a club for the devotees of a new ball-game.
nuper ad coetum me adiunxi amicorum novi folliludii.

It is called basket-ball because the object of the game is to throw the ball into the basket.	*folliculi canistrique ludus nominatur, quod follicŭlus est iaciendus in canistrum.*
It requires great skill to catch the ball, to pass it to one's team-mates, and to throw it into a basket.	*magna opus est sollertia, cum folliculus accipitur, sociis traditur, in canistrum mittitur.*
I read in the newspaper that your sister is an excellent tennis-player both outdoors and indoors.	*sororem tuam reticulo ac pila egregie ludere in actis legi diurnis cum sub divo tum in atrio.*
The tennis-court.	*sphaeristerium.*
My children play table-tennis.	*liberi mei manubriato reticulo pilulaque in mensa ludunt.*
Boys and young men are also enthusiasts for the small white ball on the green table.	*adulescentes quoque et iuvenes parvulis pilis albis super mensam viridem alliciuntur.*
To decide the championship the best players in the country meet in a serious competition.	*seria optimorum civitatis lusorum certamina de primiceriatu aguntur.*
Girls like playing volley-ball.	*puellas pila iuvat volatica ludere.*
Nowadays hockey seems to be very popular with girls.	*magna in gratia puellarum ludus pilae hastili repando percussae his temporibus videtur esse.*
I intend to watch the test matches against Australia.	*seriem certaminum spectabo in quibus praemium urna cinerum plena quae nunquam fuit vocatur.*
It's anyone's guess whether the series goes to us or to our old friends and adversaries from down under.	*dubium est utrum victoria nos respiciat an Antipodas, gentem maxime amicam et adversam.*
The wicket has to be protected	*tripalium clava saligna de-*

against a red ball with a willow bat.	*fendendum est contra pĭlae iactus.*
An alert wicket-keeper.	*impiger tripalii custos.*
How's that?	*provoco!*
Out!	*hoc habet!* (*cf. Virg. A. 12, 296*).
Not out!	*stet!* / *maneat!*
Well played!	*macte virtute!*
An effective bowler.	*pilarius fortis.*
He is a cunning left-arm bowler.	*sinistra manu pilam callide intorquet.*
An all-rounder.	*in omnibus ludi partibus veterator.*
The cricket season is over.	*clava saligna cessat.*
In my retirement I intend to take up golf.	*in senio otioso me ad lusum conferam Caledonicum.*
One must learn to drive a small white ball into a hole with a variety of clubs.	*pilulam albam clavis varie cuspidatis in puteolum dirigere discendum est.*
Whether as partner or opponent my father was always a most agreeable golfing companion.	*in ludi Caledonici certaminibus vel ut conlusor vel etiam ut adversarius pater semper erat comes iucundissimus.*
An unusual game is played at Eton on St Andrew's Day.	*insolitum genus ludi fit apud Etonenses die Sanctandreana.*
The Eton Wall Game.	*ludus muralis Etonensis.*
When the Collegers play the Oppidans at the wall there is very rarely a definite result.	*cum Togati contra Oppidanos ad murum contendunt, perraro evenit certa victoria.*
This in no way diminishes the enthusiasm of the spectators who despite mud and rain flock to a contest which is almost unintelligible and scarcely worth watching.	*quod haudquaquam minuit studia spectantium qui quamquam imbre lutoque aspersi confluunt ad certamen quod vix intelligi potest neque prorsus dignum est quod spectes.*

(b) WATER SPORTS	*(b) DE LUDICRIS AQUARIIS*
Do you also go in for water sports?	*aquariis quoque exerceris ludicris?*
I enjoy swimming events, but restrict myself to the rôle of enthusiastic spectator.	*valde certaminibus natatoriis faveo, sed spectantis tantum ago partes studiosi.*
I like the great variety of events.	*varietate delector certaminum.*
To swim breast-stroke.	*ranae more natare.*
To swim back-stroke.	*supino corpore natare.*
To swim butterfly-stroke.	*papilionum more natare.*
To swim the crawl.	*alternis bracchiis natare.*
To swim free-style.	*genere sponte delecto* (*vel norma nulla*) *natare.*
High diving.	*ars de suggestu* (*vel de turri*) *in aquam sollerter se praecipitandi.*
The climax of the entertainment is usually the water polo.	*spectaculi culmen plerumque folliculi certamen est a natantibus pulsati.*
Aren't you interested in rowing?	*nonne remigandi arti faves?*
I was once a member of a rowing club.	*remĭgum circulo interfui.*
Then you know all about it.	*ergo peritus es huius artis.*
Do you enjoy punting too?	*placet-ne etiam conto trudere cumbam?*
I practically live on the water.	*aquam vera caritate amplector.*
During the summer we row once a week.	*octavo quoque die aestatis remis navigare solemus.*
Among the boats we have an eight.	*inter alia navigia naviculam ab octo remigibus motam habemus.*
In previous years I often rowed in a coxed four.	*sŭperioribus annis navicula quattuor remigum cum gubernatore saepe vehebar.*

One of our oarsmen left for Canada yesterday and isn't coming back.	*unus ex nostris remigibus heri ad Canadam profectus est ibique manebit.*
Would you like to take his place?	*nonne hunc locum vacuum explere vis?*
Very much so.	*libenter explebo.*
But we're all very keen and don't want to lose in the regatta.	*omnes autem ambitiosi sumus neque certamine navicularum vinci volumus.*
That goes without saying.	*nimirum.*
In that case I'll have to train very hard when I join your club.	*ergo in societatem vestram adscripto mihi funditus est exercitandum.*
When can I come?	*quando te visitare mihi permissum erit?*
Come to the club-house tomorrow.	*cras in domicilium nostrum venias!*
You'll find many of our members there at nine o'clock.	*nona hora multos societatis nostrae socios (vel sodales) ibi videbis.*
Fine. I'll be there.	*bene est! Veniam.*
You won't be there yourself, will you?	*num tu quoque aderis?*
I'm not sure.	*hoc non certo scio.*
Very likely I'll come along later because I have an important letter to write beforehand.	*verisimile est me postero tempore esse venturum, quia antea epistula necessaria mihi est scribenda.*
In that case I could perhaps fetch you from your flat.	*ergo mihi fortasse venia est tui e domicilio abducendi.*
Of course.	*venia est.*
Do you know where I live?	*scisne, ubi habitem?*
Yes, I've been there once.	*scio, nam apud te iam fui.*
Please come to my place at ten o'clock; then we can go to the club-house together.	*decima hora ad me quaeso veni; quo facto una in domicilium remigum ibimus.*

You'll soon be a distinguished oarsman.	*mox in ludis fluvitialibus eminebis.*
Good-bye.	*vale!*

(c) ATHLETICS — (*c*) *DE ATHLETICA*

The hundred-metre race.	*cursus certamen centum metrorum.*
The relay-race.	*curriculum quattuor cursorum alternorum.*
The Marathon.	*cursus Marathonius.*
The long-distance runner.	*qui longa spatia percurrit.*
The hurdle-race.	*cursus impedimentorum interpositorum.*
To hurdle.	*super crātes saltu cursorio se proicere.*
The long jump.	*saltus in longitudinem.*
The high jump.	*saltus in sublime.*
The pole vault.	*saltus hastīli (vel pertĭca) factus.*
The decathlon.	*decāthlum.*
The modern pentathlon.	*pentāthlum nostrae aetatis.*
Throwing the discus, hammer, javelin.	*disci, mallei, iaculi iactus.*
A great runner.	*vir velocis plantae gloria illustris (cf. Juv. 13, 98).*
Let's not forget the athletes whose arms have been so strengthened by continual practice that they can lift the heaviest weights, snatch them from the floor and hold them up in the air.	*ne obliviscamur athletas, quorum lacerti diutina exercitatione adeo firmati sunt, ut maxima pondera leventur, a solo rapiantur, sursum tollantur.*

(d) BOXING AND WRESTLING — (*d*) *DE PUGILATU ET LUCTATIONE*

Have you ever seen a boxing match from the ringside?	*spectavistine iam pugilatum e propinquo?*

No, only on television.	*non vidi nisi in scrinio televisifico.*
Would you like to come with me to the stadium tomorrow?	*visne cras in amphitheatrum me comitari?*
What's on there?	*quid rei ibi erit?*
The best boxers of almost every class will appear in the ring.	*optimi omnium fere classium pugĭles in saepta intrabunt.*
Have you got tickets already?	*habesne iam tesseras?*
With difficulty I got two from a friend who is a member of the athletic club.	*aegre per amicum, qui sodalis coetus athletici est, duas tesseras accepi.*
Will there be a championship bout too?	*etiamne videbimus certamen de principatu pugilatorio?*
Two heavyweights, a Finn and a German, will be fighting for the European championship.	*duo magno pondere viri, Finnus et Germanus, de principatu Europaeo certabunt.*
Are they well matched in speed and punching power?	*paresne sunt adversarii agilitate ac pulsandi vi?*
The Finn is notorious for his hard punching, but the German is quicker on his feet and has greater powers of endurance.	*Finnus durissimis plagis famosus est, sed Germanus versatilior et pertinacior.*
An upper-cut.	*ictus mento immissus.*
Knocked out.	*ictū ultimo confectus.*
The referee will be a well-known ex-boxer.	*saeptorum iudex erit pugil pristĭnus notissimus.*
Boxing gloves.	*caestūs.*
There are also many wrestling fans, particularly among the young.	*etiam luctationis studio multi ardent, imprimis adulescentes.*
In ancient Greece wrestling took place in the palaestra.	*apud Graecos palaestra locus erat luctandi.*
I prefer free-style bouts to those in Greco-Roman style.	*mihi certamina Graecorum et Romanorum more minus quam, quae sunt nullius normae, placent.*

The attacker often shows remarkable speed and cunning to take his opponent by surprise and throw him on the ground.

admirabiles saepe agilitas atque calliditas sunt, quibus usus qui aggreditur adversarium opprimit et prosternit.

The attacker often shows remarkable speed and cunning to take his opponent and throw him on the ground

(e) HORSE RACING

(*e*) *DE CERTAMINE CURSUS EQUESTRIS*

The greatest happiness for Jack is sitting on a horse's back.

sedére in equí sellá nil púlchrius ín terrá.

Do you often go to race meetings?

isne saepe spectatum equirria? (*Ov. Fast.* 2, 859).

While I lived in London, I rarely missed a meeting.

dum Londinii eram, omnibus fere aderam cursibus.

It's remarkable how quickly horseracing recovered after the last war.

mire, quam celeriter equitandi ars post bellum proximum effloruerit.

In England there are a number of stud-farms where thoroughbreds are reared and trained.	*in Anglia complures sunt equariae illustres, quibus generosi equi educantur atque instituuntur.*
We also have excellent jockeys with more than a hundred victories to their credit.	*sessores quoque insignes habemus, qui plus centies vicerunt.*
I once saw a trotting race at Windsor; the horses were harnessed to light two-wheeled carriages.	*Vindelisorae aliquando equestria certamina tolutim currentium (Fronto ad M. Caes. 1, 8), qui ad cisia levia iuncti erant, spectavi.*
I once saw a four-horse chariot race in Greco-Roman style in an American circus.	*quadrigarum certamen more Graecorum et Romanorum antiquorum puer in circo quodam Americano ipse vidi.*
Races of this kind can sometimes be seen in the cinema.	*tales cursus nonnumquam ostenduntur in cinematographēis.*
Abroad too British jockeys are brilliantly successful.	*etiam extra Britanniam equites Britannici victorias pepererunt clarissimas.*
A feature of horseracing is the betting which occurs both on and off the course.	*ad equirria etiam sponsiones, quae non solum a spectantibus, sed etiam fiunt ab absentibus, pertinent.*
The tote.	*ubi praemia sponsionum distribuuntur.*
The stake.	*pignus.*

(f) GYMNASTICS — *(f) DE REBUS GYMNICIS*

Where are you off to in such a hurry?	*quo properas?*
To take part in our club's gymnastic exercises.	*ad exercitationes gymnicas societatis nostrae.*

Your badge shows that you are a member of the General Gymnastic Club.	*insigne vestrum te sodalem Communis Societatis Palaestricae esse probat.*
We meet in the gymnasium every Monday at seven o'clock in the evening.	*singulis lunae diebus vesperi hora septima in palaestram convenimus gymnasii.*
What exercises do you perform?	*quo modo exercetis corpora?*
We use the horizontal bar, the parallel bars, the rings and the horse much as we used to at school.	*tigno ferreo (vel tigno transverso), tignis parallēlis, anŭlis (vel circŭlis), equo (vel ĕcŭlĕō) similiter ac quondam in schola utimur.*
You are said to have been the best gymnast in your class.	*optimus vestrae classis palaestrīta fuisse diceris.*
Didn't you prefer gym to lessons?	*nonne libentius corpus exercuisti quam didicisti?*
I was a mediocre gymnast who preferred to jump over a table or clamber up a pole or the rungs of a ladder to attempting anything dangerous.	*ego palaestrita mediocris eram, qui mensam transilire aut manibus longurium vel scalae gradus ascendere quam res periculosas audēre malebam.*
We also do P.T. either individually or in groups.	*liberas quoque exercitationes facimus, singillātim vel per manipŭlos.*
Rhythmical gymnastic exercises.	*ludi gymnici rhythmice facti.*
Of course we have a team that trains enthusiastically for matches.	*manum videlicet habemus, quae ad certamina se parat studiose.*

(g) OTHER FORMS OF SPORT	*(g) DE ALIIS REBUS AGONISTICIS*
I go hiking.	*corpus exerceo migrando.*
Youth hostel.	*deversorium adulescentium.*
Fencing.	*ludus gladiatorius (vel studium gladiatorium).*
A fencing bout.	*certamen (vel spectaculum) battuendi (vel gladiatorium).*
The rules of fencing	*vitandi atque inferendi ictūs praecepta.*
Fencing-master.	*bǎttuendi (vel armorum) magister.*
Foil.	*dǒlō(n), ōnis m., rǔdǐs ferrea (Lat. 9, 35).*
Sabre.	*ēnsis falcatus (vel ǎcīnǎcēs, is m.).*
Fencing-school.	*ludus gladiatorius.*
In my opinion gliding is the sport that gives the greatest sense of achievement.	*haud scio, an pulcherrimum genus suis viribus facinora patrandi ars velivǒlo utendi sit.*
A gliding competition.	*velivolorum certamen.*
A sailing-boat.	*navigium veliferum.*
A sailing regatta.	*navigiorum velis instructorum certamen (Lat. 9, 31).*
A motorised sailing-boat.	*veliferum navigium automatarium.*
A yacht.	*celox, ōcis m.* and *f.*
Cycling.	*studium (vel ars) birota (vel ocypede) vehendi.*
Cyclist	*birotularius* (not: *cyclista!*).
Cycling race (between individuals or teams).	*birotulariorum certamen (inter singulos aut per manipulos).*
Road-racing (between individuals or teams).	*certamen singulorum aut manipulorum via cursitantium.*
A six-day event.	*certamen sex dierum.*

Motor-car racing.	*autoraedarum certamen.*
A racing driver.	*autoraedarum auriga* (*vel agitator*).
Motorcycle racing (with side-car).	*automatariarum birotarum* (*vel autobirotarum*) *certamen* (*cum adiecto cisio*).
Shooting.	*ars armis ignivomis utendi.*
Rifle.	*manuballista ignivoma* (*vel ignifera*).
Pistol.	*manuballistula* (*ignivoma*) (*vel pyroballistula*).
Marksman.	*manuballistarius* (*vel pyroballistarius*).
Sighting telescope.	*telescopium.*
Cartridge.	*pyrŏbolus* (*vel pyrobolum, tubulus displodens vel pyricus*).
To set the sights correctly.	*specŭlam* (*vel dioptram, visorium*) *recte ordinare* (*vel temperare*).
To shoot.	(*telum*) *emittere.*
A shooting club.	*manuballistariorum sodalitas.*
A sports paper	*ephemĕris gymnastica.*
The Sunday sports section.	*certamina lusoria hesterno die Saturni facta.*

(h) THE WINTER OLYMPICS — (*h*) *DE OLYMPIIS HIBERNIIS*

Did you see the last winter Olympics on television?	*vidistine proxima olympia hiberna per scrinium televisifĭcum?*
The pictures were perfectly magnificent.	*magnificentissima erant, quae album televisifĭcum ostendit.*
The skiers in the downhill race aroused admiration as they glided down the slopes towards their goal.	*admiratione iam digni erant cursores, qui descensu simplĭci per nives soleis oblongis ad terminum delabebantur.*

The competitors in the slalom had a harder task as they had to wind their way through a series of gates marked by small flags.	*difficilius erat certamen eorum, qui itinere flexuoso portas vexillis parvis notatas percurrere debebant.*
Skis.	*solĕae oblongae (vel Norvegicae).*
The slalom.	*descensus flexuosus.*
The giant slalom.	*ingens descensus flexuosus.*
The (great) cross-country race.	*(longus) cursus campester.*
The ski relay race.	*antecessorum cursus.*
Ski jumping.	*saltus de suggestu desultorio.*
The Nordic combination (cross-country and ski-jump).	*coniuncta exercitatio septentrionalis.*
The funicular railway.	*transmissio (vel transvectio) fūnālis (vel funivĭa).*
Chair-lift.	*pegma (-ătis, n.) sellarium (vel sellula tractoria).*
I also enjoyed very much the competitions on the ice.	*certamina, quae glaciata in planitie fiebant, mihi valde placebant.*
The Ice Stadium with room for many thousands of spectators.	*stadium glaciale, multa milia capiens sessorum.*
The skaters.	*lusores solĕis ferrĕis (vel ferratis) currentes.*
The figure-skating competition.	*certamen ferrearum solearum artificiosum.*
It is remarkable with what skill the skaters glide over the ice in time to the music.	*mirum, quanta sollertia cursores super glaciem ad symphonĭae concentum labantur.*
They describe a great variety of figures, whirl round in pirouettes and leap into the air most artistically.	*schemata maxime varia descrībunt, saltant altero pede se circumvolventes, sursum saliunt singulari arte.*
Voluntary exercises are rated as	*voluntariae exercitationes a*

highly by the judges as compulsory ones. — *certaminis iudicibus tantidem aestimantur quanti praeceptae.*

The pairs skating together draw rapturous applause from the public. — *plausūs clamoresque vir et mulier conciunctim in glacie saltantes excitant.*

Speed skating over various distances. — *celeritatis certamina, quae imparibus spatiis conficiuntur.*

Dirigible bobsleds with steering wheels and brakes. — *trahae gubernabiles et rotis moderatricibus atque sufflaminibus instructae.*

Ice-hockey. — *pilae baculique adunci ludicrum super glaciem (vel pilamallĕus).*

Atomic Power	**di vi atomica**
What greater, or should I say more terrible, discovery has been made in the twentieth century than atomic power?	*saeculo vicesimo quid maius detectum est, an dicam immanius quam vis atomica?*
Both are true, but it's clear that the physicists were only concerned to discover the structure of the atom.	*verum est utrumque; sed physicos nihil nisi id studuisse, ut atŏmorum structuram cognoscerent, apertum est.*
And we were amazed when we learned of what tiny pebbles the universe was composed.	*atque nos obstupuimus, cum, quantulis ex lapillulis mundi opus esset compositum, audivissemus.*
Do you remember people's horrified reaction when the news came over the radio that two atomic bombs had been dropped on Japan?	*meministine, quantopere homines, cum duos pyrobŏlos atomicos in urbes Iaponicas esse deiectos radiophonice nuntiaretur, perhorruerint?*
And since then the explosive force of atomic bombs has continued to grow and grow.	*atque illo ex tempore displodendi robur pyrobolorum atomicorum magis magisque auctum est.*
Did you read in the paper that the Americans have stockpiled no fewer than 50,000 atomic warheads?	*legistine in actis diurnis Americanos non minus quam quinquaginta milia displosivorum capitum atomicorum acervavisse?*
And no-one knows how many other states have collected.	*neque quisquam scit, quantum aliae civitates contulerint.*
The treaty banning the testing of nuclear weapons.	*pactum, quo convēnit, ne pyroboli atomici experimenti causa (in terrae solo supraque) dirumperentur.*
This treaty has not been signed by all countries.	*id pactum non ab omnibus civitatibus est subscriptum.*
There's good news about the	*laetabiles sunt nuntii de magnis*

great benefits that nuclear power offers to mankind.

emolumentis, quae vi atomica hominibus praebentur, divulgati.

Electrical power is produced by splitting the atom.

vis electrica scissis ex atomis comparatur.

Aircraft-carriers and submarines are supplied with nuclear power.

naves aeroplănophŏrae et navigia subaquanea vi atomica instruuntur.

Doctors use so-called isotopes for the diagnosis of disease and, for example, to heal cancer and tumours of the larynx.

medici isotŏpis, qui vocantur, ad morbos cognoscendos et, ut exemplum afferam, ad cancrum ac guttur tumidum sananda utuntur.

In almost all countries nuclear power-stations are being

in omnibus fere civitatibus officinae atomico robori ad

O for the wings of a dove

built for peaceful purposes.

pacis utilitates gignendo exstruuntur.

The Conquest of the Air

de āëre potiŭndo

'O for the wings of a dove' is what men dreamed and sang in days gone by.

'O utinam volucris pennis pernicibus essem', sic antiquitus somniabant cantabantque homines.

But no-one has yet succeeded in lifting himself from the ground into the air using the power of his own muscles.

neque vero adhuc cuiquam, ut suis musculorum viribus ex solo se in āera tolleret, contigit.

For two centuries men of courage have been flying longer or shorter distances in gas-filled balloons.

iam per duo saecula viri audaces globis panno cumoso intentis et gaso completis volabant super spatia breviora vel longiora.

These were the first aeronauts.

ii erant aeronautae primi.

The dirigible airships named after Count Zeppelin were also lighter than air.

āere leviores erant etiam aerinaves a Comite Zeppelin appellatae.

Even today small airships of this kind can be seen flying over towns advertising some commodity or other.

etiamnunc talia aerinavigia parva mercis cuiuspiam divulgandae causa super urbes volantia videntur.

Hardly seventy years have passed since skilled engineers constructed the first mechanically propelled aeroplanes.

vix anni septuaginta praeterierunt, ex quo machinariis doctis contigit, ut velivola, quae machinamentis motoriis impelluntur, construerent.

Monoplane – Biplane.

monoplănum – biplănum.

Air forces, air fleets.

arma aeria, classes aeriae.

Reconnaissance flight.	*volatus exploratorius.*
Warplane.	*aeroplănum proeliare.*
Air-raid.	*aeroplanorum incursio.*
Radar.	*radioelectricum instrumentum exploratorium.*
Civilian air traffic is primarily the concern of the airlines and proceeds according to a time table.	*civile commercium āerium imprimis societatibus aeriis sustentatur et secundum horarium peragitur.*
Every year the airline network becomes denser, and the number of passengers goes up and up.	*aeriorum itinerum rete in annos fit densius, numerus vectorum aeriorum maior et maior.*
In recent years piston-driven aircraft have been joined by others powered by turboprop or jet-propelled engines.	*proximis annis ad aeroplăna, quorum machinamenta fundulis ambulatilibus propelluntur, alia accesserunt, quae vel turbineo helicarum motu incitantur vel contraria vi propelluntur.*
A jet-aircraft.	*āeróplanum āerihaustorium* (*Pal. Lat. 34, 309*).
Recently I flew by helicopter to Bath.	*nuper helicoptĕro Aquas Sulis volavi* (*vel autogȳro*).
I've often seen such aeroplanes taking off vertically.	*saepe talia aeroplăna ad perpendiculum exsurgentia videbam.*
And man wishes to ascend higher and higher.	*altius quoque altiusque homo ascendere vult.*
In our own time one of man's oldest dreams, that of passing through the troposphere and the stratosphere into the vastness of space, has been realised.	*nostra aetate vetustissimum hominum somnium per troposphaeram et stratosphaeram in sidereum spatium immensum progrediendi ad effectum adducitur.*
Not only have unmanned capsules reached the moon on a	*non modo compluries inanes capsulae metallinae ad lunam*

number of occasions, but in recent years four pairs of brave Americans have set foot on its surface, and after spending some hours or days there have returned safely to earth.

pervenerunt, sed proximis annis quattuor paria Americanorum audacissimorum in eius superficie pedes posuerunt et nonnullas horas vel dies ibi versati incolumes reverterunt ad terram.

The Royal Family — **de Regia Domo**

The Queen. — *Elizabeth II dei gratia Britanniarum regnorumque suorum ceterorum regina consortionis populorum* (= the commonwealth) *princeps fidei defensor.*

Three cheers for Her Majesty the Queen! — *vocem vivam tollite indicem vestrarum erga augustissimam reginam nostram voluntatum ac studiorum.*

God save the Queen! — *vivat regina!*

H.R.H. Prince Philip, Duke of Edinburgh. — *Princeps celsissimus, Philippus dux Edinensis.*

H.R.H. the Prince of Wales. — *Carŏlus, celsissimus princeps Valliae.*

H.R.H. Princess Anne. — *Principissa celsissima Anne.*

The Peerage, Baronetage and Knightage — **de gradibus nobilitatis**

Duke (Duchess). — *dux* (*ducissa*).

Marquis (Marchioness). — *marchio* (*marchionissa*).

Earl (Countess). — *comes* (*comitissa*).

Baron (Baroness).	*baro* (*baronissa*).
Baronet (Lady).	*baronettus* (*domina*).
Knight Bachelor.	*eques auratus.*
Knight of the Garter (KG).	*nobilissimi ordinis Periscelidis eques.*
Knight of the Thistle (KT).	*antiquissimi et nobilissimi ordinis Cardui eques.*

Military and Civil Decorations	**de ornamentis militaribus et civilibus**
Victoria (George, Military) Cross.	*cruce Victoriana* (*Georgiana, Militari*) *ornatus.*
Distinguished Service Order.	*militari insigni propter res egregie gestas ornatus.*
Mentioned in despatches.	*in commentariis imperatoriis laudatus.*
Order of Merit (OM).	*ordini insigniter meritorum adscriptus.*
Companion of Honour (CH).	*inter viros praecipue honoratos socius adscriptus.*

Politics	**de rebus politicis**
The Prime Minister.	*regni Britannici minister primus.*
The Cabinet.	*summum rerum administrandarum concilium.*
The Privy Council.	*reginae concilium privatum.*
A Member of Parliament.	*regni totius senatoribus adscriptus.*
A distinguished M.P.	*vir senatorum ordinis amplissimi inter decora numeratus.*

A Member of the House of Commons.	*in inferiore Parliamenti camera senator.*
Four times elected Member for Windsor.	*Vindelisorae nomine regni totius senator quater adscriptus.*
Father of the House.	*senatus pater.*
A hotly contested election.	*suffragiorum in certamine non impar congressus.*
Speaker of the House of Commons.	*in inferiore Parliamenti camera prolocutor.*
The House of Lords	*Domus Procerum.* *Curia omnium augustissima.*
The Lord Chancellor.	*senatus Britannici ordini superiori praepositus.*
The Conservatives.	*optimatium partes.*
The Liberals.	*liberalium partes.*
The Labour Party.	*operariorum partes.*
An Independent Member.	*senator 'nullius addictus iurare in verba magistri'* (*Horace Ep. 1, 1, 14*).
The Leader of the Opposition.	*eorum ductor qui maioris partis consiliis resistunt.*
Government Ministers.	*ministri munerum publicorum.*
Foreign Secretary.	*rerum externarum a secretis.* *rebus externis praepositus.*
Foreign Office.	*supremum consilium externis regni negotiis praepositum.*
Home Secretary.	*provinciae domesticae praepositus.*
Minister of Defence.	*patriae totius rei militari praepositus.*
Chancellor of the Exchequer.	*aerario publico praefectus.* *scaccarii cancellarius.*
Minister of Education and Science.	*institutioni publicae praepositus.*
Lord Privy Seal.	*privati sigilli custos.*
Postmaster General.	*tabellariorum praepositus administrationi.*

Minister of Health.	*sanitati tuendae praepositus.*
The President of the U.S.A.	*inter Americanos praeses foederatarum illic civitatium.*
The Secretary of State.	*liberae rei publicae Americanae a secretis.*
The U.S. Ambassador to London.	*a foederatis Americae civitatibus ad Palatium Divi Iacobi legatus.*
The United Nations (U.N.).	*unitarum nationum societas.*
The Security Council.	*securitatis orbanae custos.*
North Atlantic Treaty Organisation (N.A.T.O.).	*foedus factum ut liberi omnes populi quorum terras Oceanus Atlanticus a Boreali parte alluit mutua fide opibusque tamquam unius corporis membra inter se devinciantur.*
Nationalism.	*nimium suae gentis studium.*
Fascism.	*exaggeratum suae gentis studium.*
Nationalisation.	*bona privata publicare in usum populi.*

Some Items from the Economic and Social Spheres — nonnulla ex provinciis oeconomica et sociali

(Taken in the main from the encyclical 'Mater et Magistra', AAS 1961, pp. 401 ff.)

The whole of mankind.	*universa hominum consociatio.*
Economic circumstances.	*res oeconomicae.*
The economy.	*res oeconomica.*
A free market.	*liber mercatus.*
Economic power.	*oeconomicus potentatus.*
The unrestrained pursuit of power.	*effrenata potentatus ambitio.*

Free competition.	*libera competitorum aemulatio.*
Industry.	*machinales industriae.*
The technical sphere.	*provincia artium.*
Branches of production.	*artes bona gignentes.*
Technical progress.	*artium progressus* (*vel profectus*).
Scientific progress.	*disciplinarum profectus.*
A skilled trade.	*procuratio ab artifice gesta.*
The medium-sized, large firm.	*administratio medii, magni ordinis.*
Private concerns.	*privatorum incepta.*
Efficient methods of production.	*artes ad res gignendas* (*vel procreandas*) *aptae.*
A cooperative concern.	*inceptum oeconomicum consociatum.*
The partners.	*sodales consociati.*
Professional associations.	*societates ad professionem spectantes.*
A craftsmen's guild.	*consociatio* (*artificum*).
Insurance institutes.	*oeconomicae cautiones.*
The manager of a firm.	*moderator societatis.*
The right of private ownership (of the means of production).	*ius privati dominii* (*vel privata possessio vel privatim res possidendi*) (*ius res bonis gignendis aptas privatim possidendi*).
The social function of private ownership.	*privati dominii sociale munus* (*vel socialis ratio*).
A social problem.	*quaestio socialis.*
Social insurance.	*sociales civium cautiones* (*vel securitatis socialis rationes*).
The labour problem.	*quaestio de opificum condicione.*
The workers.	*opifices* (*vel operarii vel operae*).
The employers.	*operum conductores.*
Terms of employment.	*pactio operarum.*

Trade unions.	*opificum collegia* (*vel consociationes*).
Collective agreements.	*pactiones inter opificum et conductorum consociationes.*
A strike.	(*voluntaria*) *operis cessatio* (*vel intermissio*).
A lock-out.	*opificum exclusio laboris.*
Class-warfare.	*dimicatio alterius ordinis in alterum.*
To improve the workers' living standards.	*operariorum rationes in melius mutare.*
Profit-sharing.	*lucra participare.*
Joint ownership or management.	*consortium dominii vel curationis.*
Marxist teachings.	*Marxiana placita.*
A moderate form of socialism.	*temperata socialismi ratio.*
International Labour Office.	*gentium consilium labori ordinando.*
Ideology.	*vulgata opinionum commenta.*
The demands of the common good.	*communis boni rationes.*
Underdeveloped countries.	*regiones* (*vel civitates*) *opibus inferiores* (*vel minus bonis oeconomicis instructae*).
The hungry masses.	*multitudo famelicorum.*
On the face of the earth.	*in universa hominum communitate.*
The mutual relations of mankind.	*mutuae hominum necessitudines.*
The World Bank.	*argentaria ad omnes spectans nationes.*
Imperial Chemical Industries (I.C.I.).	*societas imperialis rerum chemicarum confectioni operata.*
British Petroleum (B.P.).	*consociatio Britannica petolearia.*

Geographical Names (non-Classical in some cases)

(a) COUNTRIES

(I = Inhabitants)

America	*America, Hesperia Transatlantica.*	I. *Americani*
Arabia	*Arabia*	I. *Arabes.*
Belgium	*Belgica*	I. *Belgae*
Britain	*Britannia*	I. *Britanni*
Canary Islands	*Insulae Fortunatae*	
China	*Serica terra* (silk: *sericum*)	I. *Seres*
Crimea	*Chersonesus Taurica*	
Denmark	*Dania*	I. *Dani*
England	*Anglia*	I. *Angli*
Finland	*Finnia*	I. *Finni*
France	*Francogallia*	I. *Francogalli*
Greece	*Graecia*	I. *Graeci*
Greenland	*Hyperborea terra*	
Ireland	*Hibernia*	I. *Hiberni*
Israel	*Iudaea*	I. *Iudaei*
Japan	*Iaponica*	I. *Iaponici*
Lapland	*Lapponia*	I. *Lappones*
Netherlands	*Hollandia*, *Batavia*	I. *Batavi*
Norway	*Norvegia*	I. *Norvegenses*
Poland	*Polonia*	I. *Poloni*
Portugal	*Lusitania*	I. *Lusitani*
Russia	*Russia*, *Sarmatia*	I. *Russi*, *Sarmates*
Scotland	*Scotia*, *Caledonia*	I. *Scoti*, *Caledones*
Spain	*Hispania*	I. *Hispani*
Sweden	*Suetia*	I. *Sueti*
Switzerland	*Helvetia*	I. *Helvetii*
Turkey	*Turcia*	I. *Turci*

Wales	*Vallia* *Cambria* }	I. *Vallenses*
West Indies	*Indiae Occidentales*	

(b) TOWNS (BRITISH ISLES)

Aberdeen. *Aberdona.*
Ambleside. *Galava.*
Bath. *Aquae Sulis.*
Birmingham. *Birminghamia.*
Buxton. *Aquae Arnemetiae.*
Caernarvon. *Segontium.*
Caerwent. *Venta Silurum.*
Cambridge. *Cantabrigia.*
Canterbury. *Durovernum Cantiacorum.*
Carlisle. *Luguvalium.*
Carmarthen. *Moridunum.*
Catterick. *Cataractonium.*
Chelmsford. *Caesaromagus.*
Chester. *Deva.*
Chichester. *Noviomagus.*
Cirencester. *Corinium.*
Colchester. *Camulodunum.*
Doncaster. *Danum.*
Dorchester. *Durnovaria.*
Dover. *Dubris f.*
Droitwich. *Salinae.*
Dublin. *Eblana.*
Durham. *Dunelmum.*
Edinburgh. *Edina.*
Eton. *Etona.*
Exeter. *Isca Dumnoniorum.*
Gloucester. *Glevum.*
Harrow. *Herga.*
Leeds. *Ledesia.*
Leicester. *Ratae.*
Lincoln. *Lindum.*
Llandovery. *Alabum.*
London. *Londinium.*
Manchester. *Mancunium.*
Monmouth. *Blestium.*
Neath. *Nidum.*
Newcastle. *Pons Aelius.*
Nottingham. *Nottinghamia.*
Oxford. *Oxonia.*
Peterborough. *Petriburga.*
Reading. *Redinga.*
Rochester. *Durobrivae.*
St Albans. *Verulamium.*
St Andrews. *Sanctandrea.*
Salisbury. *Sarisberia.*
Sheffield. *Sefeldia.*
Shrewsbury. *Salopia.*
Staines. *Pontes.*
Wigan. *Coccium.*
Winchester. *Venta Belgarum.*
Windsor. *Vindelisora.*
Worcester. *Vigornia.*
Wroxeter. *Viroconium.*
York. *Eboracum.*

(c) OTHER TOWNS

Aachen. *Aquisgranum.*
Aix-en-Provence. *Aquae Sextiae.*
Aleppo. *Beroea.*
Amiens. *Samarobriva.*
Amsterdam. *Amstelodamum.*
Antwerp. *Antverpia.*
Arles. *Arelate.*
Augsburg. *Augusta Vindelicorum.*
Barcelona. *Barcĭno.*
Belgrade. *Belgradum. Alba Graeca.*
Berlin. *Berolinum.*
Bologna. *Bononia.*
Bonn. *Bonna.*
Boulogne. *Bononia Gallica.*
Bordeaux. *Burdigăla.*
Bratislava. *Posōnium.*
Brindisi. *Brundisium.*
Brussels. *Bruxellae.*
Cadiz. *Gades-ium. f.*
Caen. *Cadomum.*
Calais. *Calētum.*
Cologne. *Colonia Agrippina.*
Copenhagen. *Hannia.*
Dresden. *Dresda.*
Düsseldorf. *Dusseldorpium.*
Florence. *Florentia.*
Frankfurt. *Francofurtum,* on Main *ad Moenum,* on Oder *ad Oderam.*
Geneva. *Genăva, Genĕva.*
The Hague. *Haga Comitum.*
Hamburg. *Hammaburgum.*
Hannover. *Hannovera.*
Harvard. *Cantabrigia Transatlantica.*
Heidelberg. *Heidelberga.*
Jaffa. *Ioppe.*
Jerusalem. *Hierosolўma, orum n.*
Innsbrück. *Aenipons.*
Karlovy Vary (Karlsbad). *Thermae Carolinae.*
Kiel. *Kilonium.*
Leipzig. *Lipsia.*
Leningrad. *Petropolis.*
Liège. *Leodium.*
Lisbon. *Lisbōna. Olisīpo, onis f.*
Lyons. *Lugdunum.*
Madrid. *Madrītum.*
Mainz. *Moguntiăcum.*
Marseilles. *Massilia.*
Messina. *Messāna.*
Milan. *Mediolanum.*
Modena. *Mutina.*
Moscow. *Moscovia.*
Munich. *Monachium.*
New York. *Eboracum Novum.*
Nice. *Nicaea.*
Nîmes. *Nemausus f.*
Nuremberg. *Norimberga.*
Orleans. *Cenabum.*
Padua. *Patavium.*
Palermo. *Panormus.*
Paris. *Lutetia.*
Potsdam. *Postampium.*
Prague. *Praga.*
Reggio di Calabria. *Rhegium.*

Rheims. *Remi.*
Rimini. *Arimĭnum.*
Salzburg. *Iuvavum.*
Stockholm. *Holmia.*
Strasbourg. *Argentoratum.*
Stuttgart. *Stutgardia.*
Tivoli. *Tibur, ŭris, n.*
Toulouse. *Tolōsa.*
Trier. *Augusta Trevirorum.*
Trieste. *Tergeste, is, n.*
Turin. *Augusta Taurinorum*
Venice. *Venetiae.*
Versailles. *Versaliae.*
Vienna. *Vindobona.*
Warsaw. *Varsavia.*
Xanten. *Vetera.*

(d) MORE GEOGRAPHY (BRITISH)

Seas

The English Channel	*Oceănus Britannicus*
The Straits of Dover	*Fretum Gallicum*

Islands

Anglesey	*Mona Insula*
Inner Hebrides	*Ebudae Insulae*
Isle of Man	*Monapia Insula*
Isle of Mull	*Malaius Insula*
Isle of Skye	*Scitis Insula*
Isle of Wight	*Vectis Insula*
The Orkneys	*Orcades Insulae*
The Shetlands	*Thule Insula*

Rivers and Estuaries

Avon	*Abona Flumen*
Clyde	*Clota Fl.*
Dee	*Deva Fl.*
Exe, Usk	*Isca Fl.*
Forth	*Bodotria Fl.*
Humber	*Abus Fl.*
Mersey	*Seteia Fl.*
Ribble	*Belisama Fl.*
Severn	*Sabrina Fl.*

Solway Firth	*Ituna Aestuarium*
Tay	*Tava Fl.*
Thames	*Tamesis Fl.*
The Wash	*Metaris Aest.*
Ystwyth	*Estuctia Fl.*

Headlands

Cape Wrath	*Tarredum Promontorium*
Flamborough Head	*Ocelli Prom*
Land's End	*Belerium Prom.*
St David's Head	*Octapitarum Prom.*
South Foreland	*Cantium Prom.*

(e) OTHER SEAS, LAKES, RIVERS

Adriatic Sea	*Mare Adriaticum*
Aegean Sea	*Mare Aegaeum*
Atlantic Ocean	*Oceănus Atlanticus*
Baltic Sea	*Mare Balticum*
Black Sea	*Pontus Euxinus*
Caspian Sea	*Mare Caspium*
Lake Como	*Lacus Larius*
Lake Constance	*Lacus Brigantinus*
R. Danube	*Danuvius. Ister* (in the lower reaches)
R. Dnieper	*Borysthĕnes, m.*
R. Dniester	*Tyras, -ae, m.*
R. Don	*Tanais, m.*
R. Dordogne	*Duranius*
R. Douro	*Durius*
R. Drave	*Drāvus*
R. Ebro	*Ibērus*
R. Elbe	*Albis, m.*
R. Ems	*Amisia, m.*
Lake Garda	*Lacus Benācus*
R. Garonne	*Garumna, m.*
Lake Geneva	*Lacus Lemānus*

R. Guadalquivir	*Baetis -is, m.*
R. Isère	*Isăra, m.*
R. Loire	*Lĭger, Ligĕris, m.*
Lago Maggiore	*Verbanus lacus*
Mediterranean Sea	*Mare Internum*
R. Moselle	*Mosella*
R. Nile	*Nilus*
North Sea	*Mare Germanicum*
R. Oder	*Odera* or *Viadrus*
R. Rhine	*Rhenus*
R. Rhône	*Rhodanus*
R. Save	*Savus*
R. Seine	*Sequăna*
R. Tagus	*Tagus*
R. Tiber	*Tiberis*
R. Vistula	*Vistŭla*
R. Volga	*Rha* (Indeclinable)
R. Weser	*Visurgis, m.*

Proverbial Expressions

Well begun is half done.	*dimidium facti qui bene coepit habet.*
To make the best of a bad job.	*vultu ridere invito* (*Hor. Od. 3, 11, 22*).
To kill two birds with one stone.	*uno saltu duos apros capere* (*Plaut. Cas. 2, 8, 40*) or *duo parietes de eadem fidelia dealbare* (*Cic. Fam. 7, 29, 2*).
That was a godsend for him.	*hic sibi hereditatem venisse arbitratus est* (*Cic. Verr. 4, 62*).
To make a mountain out of a molehill.	*arcem ex cloaca facere* (*Cic. Planc. 95*).
To throw in the towel.	*hastas abicere* (*Cic. Mur. 45*).

To handle with kid gloves.	*molli bracchio tractare* (*cf. Cic. Att.* 2, 1, 6).
To swim against the tide.	*contra torrentem bracchia dirigere* (*Juv.* 4, 89).
While there's life there's hope.	*nondum omnium dierum sol occidit* (*Liv.* 39, 26, 9).
He stands there like a duck in a thunderstorm.	*aqua haeret!* (*Cic. Off.* 3, 117).
He's got a screw loose.	*ellebŏro indĭget.*
To be a stick-in-the-mud.	*in luto haerere* (*Plaut. Pers.* 4, 3, 66).
Practice makes perfect.	*usus est magister optimus.*
To say the first thing that comes into one's head.	*garrire quidquid in buccam venit* (*Cic. Att.* 1, 12, 4; 12, 1, 2).
Birds of a feather flock together.	*pares cum paribus facillime congregrantur* (*Cic. Sen.* 3).
In wine is truth.	*in vino veritas* (*cf. Alcaeus fr.* 57 *Bergk*).
A rare bird.	*alba avis* (*Cic. Fam.* 7, 28, 2).
He knows next to nothing.	*nec natare nec litteras novit.*
I'm going to talk to you like a Dutch uncle.	*tuis te pingam coloribus.*
One's as bad as the other.	*eandem cantilenam canunt.* *unum quom noris omnis noris* (*Ter. Phor.* 2, 1, 35). *ab uno disce omnes* (*cf. Virg. A.* 2, 65 *f.*).
Like master, like man.	*qualis rex, talis grex* (*mediaeval; cf. Petron.* 58).
Strength in numbers.	*cedendum multitudini.*
The labourer is worthy of his hire.	*par praemium labōri.*
To turn black into white.	*nigra in candida vertere* (*Juv.* 3, 29).
He takes the line of least resistance.	*multi laboris non est plerumque.*

Mind your own business!	*tuam ipse terram calca.*
You can't make a silk purse out of a sow's ear.	*non e quovis ligno fit Mercurius (Apul. Mag. p. 302).*
A bow at a venture.	*mittere lineam (Plaut. Most. 5, 1, 27).*
To burn the candle at both ends.	*Herculi quaestum conterere (Plaut. Most. 4, 2, 73).*
To build castles in the air.	*vigilans somniare (Plaut. Capt. 4, 2, 68).*
Moderation in all things.	*medio tutissimus ibis (Ov. Met. 2, 137).*
Charity begins at home.	*tunica propior pallio (Plaut. Trin. 5, 2, 30).*
To play one's cards well.	*albo rete oppugnare (Plaut. Pers. 1, 2, 22).*
To nip in the bud.	*principiis obstare (Ov. Remed. 91).*
Coals to Newcastle.	*in silvam ligna ferre (Hor. Sat. 1. 10, 34).*
Out of one's depth.	*in alieno foro litigare (Mart. 12 Praef.).*
Hunger is the best sauce.	*cibi condimentum fames (Socrates apud Cic. Fin. 2, 90).*
Devil take the hindmost.	*occupat extremum scabies (Hor. A.P. 417).*
Familiarity breeds contempt.	*nimia familiaritas parit contemptum.*
Teach your grandmother to suck eggs.	*sus Minervam docet (Cic. Ac. Post. 1, 18).*
One good turn deserves another.	*manus manum lavat* (χεὶρ χεῖρα νίπτει, *Menand. Monost. 543).*
Dog doesn't eat dog.	*canis caninam non est (apud Varro L.L. 7, 31).*
To sit on the fence.	*naufragium ex terra intueri (Cic. Att. 2, 7, 4).*

Between two fires.	*hac urget lupus, hac canis angit* (*Hor. Sat.* 2, 2, 64).
Man's extremity is God's opportunity.	*afflictatio facit religiosos.*
The game is not worth the candle.	*piscari aureo hamo* (*Suet. Aug.* 25).
There's many a slip 'twixt the cup and the lip.	*quid vesper ferat* (*vehat*), *incertum est* (*Liv.* 45, 8, 7).
To split hairs.	*de lana caprina rixari* (*Hor. Ep.* 1, 18, 15).
To be hoist with one's own petard.	*iugulari suo gladio* (*Ter. Ad.* 5, 8, 35).
On the horns of a dilemma.	*inter sacrum saxumque stare* (*Plaut. Capt.* 3, 4, 84).
To look a gift horse in the mouth.	*equi dentes inspicere donati* (*Hieron. Prolog. in Ep. ad Eph.* 538).
Nothing venture, nothing win.	*fortes fortuna!* (*sc. adiuvat; Ter. Phorm.* 1, 4, 26 and *passim*).
You can take a horse to water, but you cannot make him drink.	*stultitia est venatum ducere invitas canes* (*Plaut. Stich.* 1, 2, 82).
Talk of the devil!	*lŭpus in fabula!* (*Ter. Ad.* 4, 1, 21).
Poacher turned gamekeeper.	*ovem lŭpo committere* (*Ter. Eun.* 5, 1, 16).
A Jack of all trades.	*omnis Minervae homo* (*Petr.* 43).
The die is cast!	*iacta alea est* (*Suet. Div. Iul.* 32). (ἀνερρίφθω κύβος *Plut. Pomp.* 60.)
The golden mean.	*aurea mediocritas* (*Hor. Od.* 2, 10, 5).
To kick against the pricks.	*adversum stimulum calcare* (*Ter. Phor.* 1, 2, 28).

All or nothing!	*aut Caesar aut nihil* (motto of Cesare Borgia around 1500).
Throw enough mud and some will always stick!	*calumniare audacter; semper aliquid haeret.*
Tell it to the Marines!	*credat Iudaeus Apella! (Hor. Sat. 1, 5, 100).*
To lock the stable door after the horse has bolted.	*sero clipeum post vulnera sumere (Ov. Tr. 1, 3, 35).*
Every cloud has a silver lining.	*inter vepres rosae nascuntur (Amm. Marc. 16, 7, 4).*
A snake in the grass.	*latet anguis in herba (Virg. E. 3, 93).*
No smoke without fire.	*semper flamma fumo proxima (Plaut. Curc. 1, 1, 53).*
Stolen fruit tastes sweetest.	*vile est quod licet (Petr. 93).*
Once in a blue moon.	*ad kalendas Graecas (Suet. Aug. 87).*
Lost Labour.	*laterem lavare (Ter. Phor. 1, 4, 8).*
You have made your bed and will have to lie on it.	*tute hoc intristi; tibi omne est exedendum (Ter. Phor. 2, 2, 4).*
You know which side your bread is buttered.	*scis uti foro (Ter. Phor. 1, 2, 29).*
To bang one's head against a brick wall.	*verberare lapidem (Plaut. Curc. 1, 3, 40).*
To have two strings to one's bow.	*duplici spe uti (Ter. Phor. 4, 2, 13).*
To err is human.	*errare humanum est (Ter. Adelph. 3, 4, 25; Cic. Verr. 5, 117).*
A storm in a teacup.	*fluctus in simpulo excitare (Cic. Leg. 3, 16, 36).*
To nourish a viper in one's bosom.	*viperam nutricare sub ala (Petr. 77).*

A man's education is never complete.	*dies diem docet* (*cf. Publil. Syrus Sent. 123*).
We learn by teaching.	*docendo discimus.*
To waste one's breath.	*emortuo verba facere* (*Plaut. Poen. 4, 2, 18*).
One learns from one's mistakes.	*expertus metuit* (*Hor. Ep. 1, 18, 87*).
Constant dripping wears away the stone.	*gutta cavat lapidem* (*Ovid. ex P. 4, 10, 5*).
One man's meat is another man's poison.	*suam cuique sponsam, mihi meam* (*Atil. apud Cic. Att. 14, 20, 3*).
There's the rub.	*hinc illae lacrimae* (*Ter. Andr. 1, 1, 29*).
There are faults on both sides.	*Iliacos intra muros peccatur et extra* (*Hor. Ep. 1, 2, 16*).
To lead up the garden path.	*montes promittere* (*sc. auri*) (*Pers. 3, 65*).
To laugh up one's sleeve.	*in sinu gaudere* (*Cic. Tusc. 3, 21, 51*).
With a pinch of salt (i.e. not literally).	*cum grano salis* (*cf. Plin. N.H. 23, 8, 77, 148*).
It never rains but it pours.	*sequitur varam vibia* (*Auson. Idyll. 12*).
Nothing in excess.	*ne quid nimis* (*Ter. Andr. 1, 1, 34*).
Cobbler, stick to your last.	*ne sutor supra crepidam* (*iudicaret*) (*Plin. N.H. 35, 10, 36, 85*).
No rose without a thorn.	*ubi uber, ibi tuber* (*Appul. Flor. 18*).

Philosophical and Legal Maxims

A good teacher is good at making distinctions.	*bene docet, qui bene distinguit.*
I think, therefore I am.	*cogito, ergo sum (Descartes).*
It is pointless to argue with one who does not accept basic principles.	*contra principia negantem non est disputandum.*
If the cause is invalid, so is the effect.	*cessante causa cessat effectus.*
Nature is greatest in the smallest things.	*natura in minimis maxima.*
There is no such thing as a vacuum.	*non datur vacuum.*
Nature makes no jumps.	*natura non facit saltus (Linnaeus).*
No rule without an exception.	*nulla regula sine exceptione.*
All that lives comes from the egg.	*omne vivum ex ovo.*
Who proves too much, proves nothing.	*qui nimium probat, nihil probat.*
Nothing comes from nothing.	*de nihilo nihil fit (cf. Lucret. 1, 150* and *Epicurus, Epist. 1, 38:* οὐδὲν γίγνεται ἐκ τοῦ μὴ ὄντος).
(Hippocrates' principle of healing.)	*contraria contrariis (sc. curantur).*
(The principle of homoeopathy).	*similia similibus.*
Ignorance of the law is no protection (sc. from punishment).	*ignorantia legis nocet.*
When two parties quarrel the third reaps the benefit.	*duobus litigantibus tertius gaudet.*
No one may be judge in his own case.	*ne quis iudex in propria causa!*

It takes at least three to form a company. — *tres faciunt collegium* (*Dig. L, 16, 85*).

What is not recorded simply does not exist. — *quod non est in actis, non est in mundo.*

The doer is the one who benefits from the deed. — *is fecit, cui prodest.*

To whose advantage? — *cui bono?* (*Cicero Mil. 12, 32*).

Tell me who your friends are, and I'll tell you who you are. — *noscitur ex sociis, qui non cognoscitur ex se.*

Many are called, but few are chosen. — *non omnes, qui habent citharum, sunt citharoedi* (*Varro R. R. 2, 1, 3; following* πολλοί τοι ναρθηκοφόροι, παῦροι δέ τε βάκχοι, *Paroemiogr. Gr. I 151, cf. Plato, Phaedo 69C*).

If only you had remained silent, your reputation would not have suffered! — *o si tacuisses, philosophus mansisses!* (*cf. Boeth. Cons. Phil. 2, 7*).

Women should remain silent in church. — *taceat mulier in ecclesia* (*1. Cor. 14, 34*).

Much ado about nothing. — *parturiunt montes, nascetur ridiculus mus* (*Hor. A. P. 139*).

Even Homer has been known to nod. — *quandōque bonus dormītat Homerus* (*Hor. A. P. 359*).

I'll show you! — *quos ego!* (*Virg. A. 1, 135*).

There are as many opinions as there are men. — *quot homines, tot sententiae* (*Ter. Phorm. 2, 4, 14; cf. Hor. Sat. 2, 1, 27*).

In time of need unity, in time of doubt freedom, at all times love. — *in necessariis unitas, in dubiis libertas, in omnibus caritas* (attributed to St Augustine).

Love conquers all. — *omnia vincit amor* (*Virg. E. 10, 69*).

In heaven's name, how long? — *quousque tandem?* (*Cic. Cat. I. init. Sall. Cat. 20, 9. Liv. 6, 18, 5*).

Without any bias.	*sine ira et studio* (*Tac. Ann. 1, 1*).
Times change, and we change with them.	*tempora mutantur, nos et* (*sic!* not: *et nos*) *mutamur in illis* (said to have originated with Emperor Lothar I).
Variety is the spice of life.	*variatio delectat* (*Cic. Nat. Deor. 1. 4, 21*).
Life is a battle.	*vivere militare est* (*Sen. Ep. 96, 5*).
Leave well alone.	*manum de tabula!* (*Plin. N. H. 35, 80*).
The show is over.	*sat prata biberunt* (*Virg. E. 3, 111*).
A word to the wise is enough.	*verbum sapienti sat* (*Plaut. Pers. 4, 7, 19. Ter. Phorm. 3, 3, 8*).
Dare to be wise.	*sapere aude* (*Hor. Epist. 1, 2, 40*).
Every man is presumed innocent until found guilty.	*quisque praesumitur bonus, donec probetur contrarium.*
Necessity knows no law.	*necessitas caret lege.*
A willing victim has no ground for complaint.	*volenti non fit iniuria.*
One witness, no witness.	*unus testis nullus testis.*
Let's hear the other side of the case.	*audiatur et altera pars* (*Seneca, Medit. 199*).
Silence is taken as consent.	*qui tacet, consentire videtur* (*Decret. V 12, 43*).
The burden of proof rests on the plaintiff.	*affirmanti occumbit comprobatio.*
The defendant must be given the benefit of the doubt.	*in dubio pro reo.*
In doubtful cases the more lenient view must be taken.	*in dubio mitius.*
The more law, the less justice.	*summum ius summa iniuria* (*Cic. Off. 1, 10, 33*).

A man may not be punished twice for the same offence.	*ne bĭs in idem* (*cf. Demosth. Lept. 147*).
Abuse does not invalidate a use.	*abusus non tollit usum.*
Possession is nine points of the law.	*beati possidentes.* (οἱ δ' ἔχοντες ὄλβιοι *Eur. frg. 326*).
Benefits cannot be forced on a man.	*beneficia non obtruduntur.*
No man's obligations extend beyond his capabilities.	*ultra posse nemo obligatur* (*Digest. L 17, 84*).
To each his own!	*suum cuique!* (*Cic. Off. 1, 5, 15*).
The good of the people is the chief law.	*salus publica suprema lex* (*est*) (*cf. Cic. de leg. 3, 3, 8*).

Some Famous Passages and Verses

The Oracle's reply to Croesus

Croesus Halym penetrans magnam pervertet opum vim.
(Κροῖσος Ἅλυν διαβὰς μεγαλὴν ἀρχὴν διαλύσει).

Virgil contrasts Greece and Rome

Excudent alii spirantia mollius aera,
Cedo equidem, vivos ducent de marmore vultus;
Orabunt causas melius caelique meatus
Describent radio et surgentia sidera dicent.
Tu regere imperio populos, Romane, memento –
Hae tibi erunt artes, – pacique imponere morem,
Parcere subiectis et debellare superbos. (*Aeneid VI, 847.*)

Tacitus explains the secret of Rome's success

Maneat quaeso duretque gentibus, si non amor nostri, at certe odium sui, quando urgentibus imperii fatis nihil iam praestare fortuna maius potest quam hostium discordiam. (*Germ. 3.3.*)

The Epitaph by Simonides on the Spartan dead at Thermopylae, in Cicero's translation.

Dic, hospes, Spartae nos te hic vidisse iacentes,
Dum sanctis patriae legibus obsequimur.

(*Tusc. 1, 42, 10.*)

Virgil's Epitaph

Mantua me genuit, Calabri rapuere, tenet nunc
Parthenope; cecini pascua, rura, duces.

(Virgil was born near Mantua, died at Brindisi in ancient Calabria and was buried in Naples, also known as Parthenope, in the *via Puteolana*. He wrote the Eclogues, Georgics and Aeneid. He is said to have written this epitaph himself shortly before his death.)

The Oracle's ambiguous reply to Pyrrhus

Aio te, Aeacida, Romanos vincere posse.

On the house where Columbus was born near Genoa

Unus erat mundus. Duo sunt, ait ille. Fuere.

Schill's Epitaph in Stralsund

(Schill's body was buried without its head.)

– Magna voluisse magnum. –
Occubuit fato. Iacet ingens litore truncus
Avolsumque caput; tamen haud sine nomine corpus.

Following Virgil's A. 2, 557 where the last line runs:

Avolsumque umeris caput et sine nomine corpus.

Royal Mottoes

The Emperor Augustus: *Festina lente.* More haste, less speed.
Edward I: *Pactum serva.* Keep faith.

Edward IV: *Modus et ordo.* Method and order.

Edward VI: *Idem per diversa.* The same whatever the circumstances.

Elizabeth I: *Semper eadem.* Always the same.

Henry II: *Utrumque.* Both (i.e. he was prepared for both peace and war).

Henry III: *Qui non dat quod habet non accipit ille quod optat.* He who does not give what he has, does not receive what he wants.

James I: *Beati pacifici.* Blessed are the peace-makers.

Richard I: *Christo duce.* Christ is my leader.

Stephen: *Vi nulla invertitur ordo.* By no force is their arrangement altered (a reference to the three ostrich plume feathers of his crest).

William II: *Perfero.* I endure.

Royal Arms of Scotland: *Nemo me impune lacessit.* No one attacks me with impunity.

Curious and Attractive Verses

Palindromic Hexameters (i.e. they read the same backwards as forwards):

Otto tenet mappam, madidam mappam tenet Otto.

Sumitis a vetitis; sitit is, sitit Eva, sitimus.

Read the other way round the following hexameter becomes a pentameter:

Adam primus homo crux omni posteritati.

(NB: the first syllable in Adam can be long or short.)

The following lines can be read either as hexameters or pentameters:

Quando nigrescit nox, rem latro patrat atrox.

Filia sub tilia nebat subtilia fila.

Sunt pueri pueri, pueri puerilia tractant.

An Elegiac Couplet in four words:

Perturbabantur Constantinopolitani
Innumerabilibus sollicitudinibus.

(Alleged) hexameter by Alarich before the gates of Rome:

Te te|ro, Ro|ma ma|nu nu|da; da|te te|la, la|tete!

When Schopenhauer heard of the death of his former housekeeper to whom he had to pay a pension for life in compensation for a physical injury which he had done her, he wrote on the envelope:

Obit anus, abit onus.

Amore, more, ore, re
Servantur amicitiae.

Laudat alauda Deum, dum sese tollit in altum;
Dum cadit in terram, laudat alauda Deum.

Famous onomatopoeic hexameters:

At tuba terribili sonitu taratantara dixit.
(*Ennius. cf. Virg. A. 9, 503.*)

Quadrupedante putrem sonitu quatit ungula campum
(*Virg. A. 8, 596. cf. 11, 875.*)

Quamvis sint sub aqua, sub aqua maledicere tentant.
(*Ov. Met. 6, 376.*)

Though submerged under the waves, submerged they still go on cursing.

LETTER ENDINGS:

Mitto tibi navem prora puppique carentem.
(the greeting: *ave.*)

Mitto tibi metulas; si vis cognoscere, vertas.
(*mētulas* (obelisks) read backwards produces *salutem.*)

PUZZLE:

O quid tua te
be bis bia abit
ra ra ra
es et in
ram ram ram
ii.

(*O super-be, quid super-bis? tua super-bia te super-abit; ter-ra es et in ter-ram i-bis.*)

A MNEMONIC:

To distinguish between *simulo* and *dissimulo*

Quae non sunt, simulo. Quae sunt, ea dissimulantur.

EPITAPH OF A DRINKER:

(Trochaic, a very jolly rhythm.)

Dum vixi, bibi libenter; bibite vos, qui vivitis!
(*Dessau, Inscript. Lat. selectae 2238.*)

THE WHOLE WORLD IN LOVE!

Cras amet, qui numquam amavit, quique amavit, cras amet!

The refrain of the *Pervigilium Veneris*. Here too the trochees have a light-hearted ring.)

FIVE REASONS FOR DRINKING:

Si bene commemini, causae sunt quinque bibendi:
Hospitis adventus, praesens sitis atque futura
Et vini bonitas et quaelibet altera causa.
(*Menagius* [*1613–1692*].)

THE BELOVED:

Si quis non vidit Venerem, quam pinxit Apelles,
pupa(m) meam adspiciat; talis et illa nitet.
(Scribbled on a wall in Pompeii,
Lommatzsch, Carm. Lat. Epigr. 2057.)

VERSES COMPOSED BY HADRIAN ON HIS DEATHBED:

Animula vagula blandula,
hospes comesque corporis,
quae nunc abibis in loca
pallidula rigida nudula,
nec ut soles dabis iocos?

ENJOYMENT OF LIFE:

Venari, lavari,
ludere, ridere,
occ (= *hoc*) *est vivere!*

(Scratched on a step in the forum at Timgad.)

Balnea, vina, Venus corrumpunt corpora nostra.
Sed vitam faciunt balnea, vina, Venus!
(*Bücheler, Carm. Lat. Epigr.* 1499.)

FAREWELL TO LIFE:

Evasi, effugi. Spes et Fortuna, valete!
Nil mihi vobiscumst. Ludificate alios!

(On a coffin in the Lateran Museum in Rome. No. 895.)

VERSUS RECIPROCI:

After the election of Pope Clement IV (1265 to 1268) the following verses circulated:

Laus tua, non tua fraus, virtus, non copia rerum
Scandere te fecit hoc decus eximium.
Pauperibus tua das, numquam stat ianua clausa,
Fundere res quaeris nec tua multiplicas.
Condicio tua sit stabilis! Non tempore parvo
Vivere te faciat hic Deus omnipotens!

The respect expressed in these lines is changed into the opposite if they are read backwards with the punctuation suitably altered:

Omnipotens Deus hic faciat te vivere parvo
Tempore! Non stabilis sit tua condicio!
Multiplicas tua nec quaeris res fundere; clausa
Ianua stat, numquam das tua pauperibus.
Eximium decus hoc fecit te scandere rerum
copia, non virtus, fraus tua, non tua laus.

The poem is also a memorial to a quite remarkable skill in the writing of Latin.

End. *finis.*